To my dear friends Jim & Susan. May your journey bring you both closer to the warm embrace of Our Lord! Love Fr. Jah

Upon an Untrodden Path

Upon an Untrodden Path

Encontering God Along The Journey

Father John J. Gordon, OMI

XULON PRESS

Xulon Press
2301 Lucien Way #415
Maitland, FL 32751
407.339.4217
www.xulonpress.com

© 2022 by Father John J. Gordon, OMI

All rights reserved solely by the author. The author guarantees all contents are original and do not infringe upon the legal rights of any other person or work. No part of this book may be reproduced in any form without the permission of the author.

Due to the changing nature of the Internet, if there are any web addresses, links, or URLs included in this manuscript, these may have been altered and may no longer be accessible. The views and opinions shared in this book belong solely to the author and do not necessarily reflect those of the publisher. The publisher therefore disclaims responsibility for the views or opinions expressed within the work.

Unless otherwise indicated, Scripture quotations taken from the Holy Bible, New International Version (NIV). Copyright © 1973, 1978, 1984, 2011 by Biblica, Inc.™. Used by permission. All rights reserved.

Paperback ISBN-13: 978-1-66285-191-9
Ebook ISBN-13: 978-1-66285-192-6

Table of Contents

Introduction vii

The First Step 1
Doors 11
Roads 23
Feet 33
Suffering Along the Journey 41
Detours Along the Journey 55
Lighting the Way 67
Food for the Journey 75
Awareness Along the Journey 83
Perseverance 93
The Interior Journey 103
Time 111
Signs 119
Companions on the Journey 129
The Final Journey 137

Introduction

"It is good to have an end to journey toward;
but it is the journey that matters, in the end."

—Ernest Hemingway

The inner prompting that led me to write this book has come from the life experiences and journeys that I have embarked upon over the years. Experiences and adventures have helped shape the way I look at my relationship with God, the world He created, and my own life. And, the many people I have encountered along this journey, include a loving family, friends, parishioners and even strangers have had a tremendous impact on my life and have helped to give shape to the person I have become. These people have also helped me navigate the road of my discernment. It is a road that has ultimately led to my increasing awareness of how much I am loved by my Lord who has called me to follow him.

I realize that not all people look at their journey through life as a spiritual one; centered on a relationship with the Divine. Many take a more earthly approach, embarking on remarkable adventures throughout the country and the world, testing their limits physically, and emotionally, and awakening within themselves a sense of meaningful fulfillment that they may have never known possible. I often think of a person summiting Mt. Everest or striving for Olympic gold or one who can compete in the Tour de France, while others test their limitations and skill, surfing the enormous waves in the waters of Nazare, Portugal.

In addition to physical accomplishments, many people seek meaning and purpose in creative pursuits. Think of the many artists, musicians, innovators, and entrepreneurs who have enriched the lives of many through their own journey of imagination, creativity, dedication, and tireless efforts.

Looking at one's life as a journey may not be an accurate metaphor for everyone, but I believe that is precisely what one's life is: a journey of becoming the person God created us to be. By sharing my own life experiences, along with stories of many whose names may be familiar to the reader, I believe this book can help inspire others and even nudge a reader or two to embark on a life-giving and enriching journey of their own. It would be a journey of awakening within oneself a world of possibilities that await all who are willing to take the first step.

Chapter One

The First Step

"A journey of a thousand miles begins with a single step."

—Laozi

Several years ago I read a remarkable book entitled *The Seven Summits* written by Dick Bass and Frank Wells. Both Wells and Bass embarked on an extraordinary journey: to summit the highest mountain peaks on each of the world's seven continents from Aconcagua in South America to Mount Everest in Asia, from Kilimanjaro in Africa to Vinson Massif in Antarctica, from Mount McKinley in North America to Elbrus in Europe, and Mount Kosciusko in Australia. As the two men embarked on this amazing adventure, they were both aware that no one in the world had ever scaled all seven summits—it would be a first, a feat that has eluded even the world's most accomplished mountaineers.

What made the feat all the more extraordinary was the fact that both Wells and Bass were businessmen, not mountaineers. Both had little if any climbing experience, and they could be ranked as novices, let alone world-class climbers, If that weren't enough, Wells was fifty-one years old, and Bass was already fifty-three when they set out. Ultimately, they put their shoulders to the plow and never looked back, accomplishing the impossible dream of conquering the seven summits! Throughout these difficult and challenging treks, Dick Bass would often repeat to himself the following quote to help him along the difficult terrain: *"Every step upon an untrodden path is a venture which only in unusual circumstances looks sensible and likely to succeed."* The quote, written by Albert Schweitzer, now hangs on the wall in my office. Like Bass, I too have it ingrained in my own memory, and it has become a constant companion on my journey of self-discovery and discernment.

Many journeys that people have embarked upon, must have been filled with that same sense of awe, excitement, anxiety, doubt, and fear.

Think about how often the disciples of Jesus lacked the faith, trust, and courage to follow where He was leading them, wondering if that journey was sensible and likely to succeed. In one passage in scripture, we even hear one of the apostles say to Jesus:

> *"Lord increase our faith." To which Jesus responds, "Truly I tell you, if you have faith as small as a mustard seed, you can say to this mountain, 'Move from here to there,' and it will move, for nothing will be impossible for you."(Matt. 17:20)*

Faith and trust in both God, oneself and the support of others are critical components in confidently taking that first step of any journey. Recall the words of one of our country's greatest leaders: "*Divine assistance arrives when the human agents of those purposes go forward and take the first steps*" *(Abraham Lincoln)*.

St. Paul, the apostle, another great leader of the church, lived a life with great faith and trust in the providential hand of God. Recall that it was St. Paul who uttered the following words that have inspired millions of Christians over the centuries to recognize the gifts and talents God has bestowed upon them, and to use those gifts and talents to meet the needs and concerns of others and for God's greater glory.

"I can do all things through Christ who strengthens me"(Phil. 4:13). Paul knew that if he was to have any impact on the world as an apostle, he had to first die to himself and allow Christ to live more fully within him. To this day, Paul's amazing displays of faith, trust, and courage continue to embolden many Christians to go beyond their comfort zones and bring the good news of the Gospel to God's people.

When I think of taking those critical first steps of becoming the person God created me to be, I often think of the steps along a pilgrimage. A pilgrimage is a spiritual journey undertaken to seek communion with God. Although some pilgrims have wandered continuously with no fixed destination, pilgrims more commonly seek a specific place that has been sanctified by God. I often think of the millions of pilgrims over the centuries who have walked the holy pilgrimage of the Camino de Santiago de Compostella in Spain (on my bucket wish list by the way). Countless millions of pilgrims over the centuries have made their way to Santiago de Compostela in the northwestern-most corner of Spain, the final destination being its famous cathedral and site of the burial of Saint James, the apostle. In the Middle Ages, the "Camino" became the leading pilgrimage destination in all of Europe. Trails led there from Germany and Poland, from Italy, Paris, and Canterbury and even from the Holy Land. St. Francis of Assisi went there not once but twice— The Spanish Camino leads from the French border and

The First Step

is as well-traveled as any pilgrimage destination in the world. Author James Michener in his book, *Iberia*, refers to it as "the finest journey in Spain and one of the two or three best in the world."

Michener describes seven different sorts of people who have traveled the famous road. "First were the devout Christians seeking salvation (and many of those, he says, being of ripe age, probably died along the way). Second were knights, usually on horseback who vowed to take the trip if they were successful in their battles.

Then there were monks, priests, and occasional cardinals for whom a visit to the tomb of a saint was the culmination of a life in the Church....Fourth were criminals, sentenced by a judge to make the trek instead of serving time. In one such story, a poor German man was sentenced by a judge for murder, to walk from Eastern Germany to Santiago and back carrying—the corpse of the man he had murdered. Hard to imagine such a sadistic sentence being handed down."

Michener continues, "Next along the route were thieves, beggars, and other unsavory characters who survived at the expense of others. Sixth, were tradesmen of every sort who sold or made whatever the hordes of pilgrims needed, including religious articles such as rosaries and scapulars. And finally there various government agents, keeping an eye out for whatever might be useful information for officials in Madrid."

Today millions of pilgrims continue the tradition on this great adventure. People make the pilgrimage for many different reasons. For most, it is a spiritual journey. However, others look at is an excellent adventure in which they will take in magnificent vistas of the Pyrenees mountains while encountering interesting people from around the world. Still, others see it as a road of repentance for some past sin or indiscretion. Whatever the motivation, many have claimed that the journey has changed them in a transformative and genuinely profound way. Michener claims that the Camino "Is the very heart of the Church in Spain."

Of course, not many people are in a financial position or may not have a window of time to make such a pilgrimage. I remember reading a story of Phil Volker, a free-spirited man living with Stage 4 Cancer, who dreamt of walking the 500-mile spiritual pilgrimage. Unable to make the trip, Phil built his own Camino in the forest behind his house on Vashon Island, Seattle. Phil, who is a veteran, husband, father, and outdoorsman, dreamed of walking the 500-mile ancient pilgrimage route across Spain. Although he knew this was an unattainable dream due to weekly chemo treatments, it did not stop him from walking. Crafting a path through the woods and pastures on his ten-acre plot of land, Phil re-created a Camino path of his own in his backyard. After each 0.88 km lap, Phil plotted his progress on a Camino map. What a remarkable story! Although Phil may never make the actual pilgrimage, I know that he is receiving some extraordinary graces and blessings for creating his own Camino.

Giving my yes to Christ required a lot of faith and trust in taking that first step, as I discerned my calling in becoming a priest with the Missionary Oblates of Mary Immaculate. Initially, I had many doubts as to whether I honestly had a vocation to religious life. Even during moments of clarity in which I felt sure of God's call, I often acted more like one of God's frozen people, rather than one of His chosen ones—frozen in place with self-doubt and a sense of being unworthy of such a calling. I felt at times like Jonah fleeing the call of God, afraid to take that first step in responding to His invitation. At other times, I resembled the rich young man of the Gospel, not willing to let go of worldly pursuits. It was only through much prayer and discernment that I began to realize more and more like St. Paul, I too needed to believe that I could indeed do all things in the one who strengthened me and that I should not fear the calling, but embrace it! That belief led me toward taking the first step of my own spiritual journey.

In the comedy film, *What About Bob?*, Bill Murray plays Bob Wiley, a man plagued with every possible phobia known to man. Bob seeks the help of well-known psychiatrist; Dr. Leo Marvin, played by Richard Dreyfus, who agrees to see Bob. Fortunately for Bob, Dr. Marvin has just written a best-selling book entitled *Baby Steps*. The concept behind baby steps is to look at one's journey in life as a series of small steps rather than massive, daunting strides filled with fear, anxiety. and peril. Bob, who is terrified of even leaving his own home, begs Dr. Marvin to help him overcome his many phobias. Without missing a beat, Dr. Marvin pulls one of his numerous copies of *Baby Steps* from the shelf in his office.

Dr. Marvin assures Bob that if he is willing to take a couple of small "baby" steps from his chair to the door of the office, to the elevator and to the streets below, he will soon realize that taking small steps in life will alleviate much of Bob's fear and anxiety. A series of hilarious events rapidly unfold, which I will not reveal. I found the movie to be both endearing and funny, with a few pearls of wisdom thrown in for good measure! Taking baby steps, at least initially, might enable a lot of people to embark on their own journey and awaken within themselves the many possibilities life has to offer.

I recommend that if you are ready to take that first step of your journey of self-discovery, adventure, purpose, and fulfilment, commit to memory some of the scriptural passages below that will remind you that you are never alone! Here are a few reminders that I have found very comforting as I continue my own journey.

> *"Walk with your feet on earth, but in your heart, be in heaven."* (St. John Bosco)

Scripture for meditation

The First Step

I will put my spirit within you, and cause you to walk in my statutes" (Ezek. 36:27).

Be strong and courageous. Do not be frightened, and do not be dismayed, for the Lord your God is with you wherever you go"(Josh. 1:9).

"And behold, I am with you always, to the end of the age"(Matt. 28:20).

Chapter Two

Doors

Behold, I have set before you an open door, which no one is able to shut" (Rev. 3:9).

In the year 2000, I was stationed at a parish in New Orleans, Louisiana. The church is known as "The International Shrine of St. Jude" and, for many years, the church was famous for its well-attended novenas to St. Jude Thaddeus, the patron saint of hopeless causes. I was in the middle of my diaconate year on the final stretch toward my ordination to the priesthood. It was a special time to be assigned to this historic parish, as it was the beginning of a new century and a new millennium (2000). In the church, it was the Year of Jubilee proclaimed by Pope John Paul II. It was Pope John Paul II who uttered the famous phrase, "*Do not be afraid. Open, I say open wide the doors for Christ!*" Pope John Paul II began his own pontificate in 1977 with those same words. Was it a clarion call to allow Jesus to enter more deeply into our lives? The phrase would become a centerpiece for this profound and sacred year of Jubilee in the church.

In the Gospel, Jesus states, *"I am the door; if anyone enters by me, he will be saved and will go in and out and find pasture" (John 10:9).* Jesus explains that He has come so that those who believe in Him *"may have life and have it abundantly,"* A beautiful promise for those who enter this sacred door! To enter through the door is to enter into true life, that is, the Triune God's eternal life of love. Later in the Gospel, Jesus declares, *"I am the way, and the truth, and the life; no one comes to the Father, but through me" (John 14:6).*

The image of the door and other symbols of entry and exit are found throughout the scriptures. These images are often used as an invitation to enter into a deeper and more life-giving relationship with God. The catechism uses the image of a door in describing the sacrament of baptism: "Holy Baptism is the basis of the whole Christian life, the door to life in the Spirit *(vitae spiritualis ianua),* and the door which gives access to the other sacraments."

In her thought provoking book, *Open Door: A journey to the true self*, author and religious Sr. Joyce Rupp O.S.M. writes the following:

Every moment is a doorway, a promise of revelation, elation. Doors to the sacred are waiting for our knock. If we give due attention and do not run from what repels or brings us pain, we unearth a wealth of knowledge and inspiration. We find our way home.

The inner door the author is speaking about, is the human heart, which needs to be open to receive God and our brothers and sisters into our lives. In another passage, Rupp writes: "I invite you to open (and close) your inner door to discover and live more fully your tremendous potential of God-ness. As you reflect and pray, may this process lead you to your authentic self."

The Light of the World by William Holman Hunt is a famous painting Hunt completed in 1853. The painting hangs to this day in Keble College, Oxford. The painting depicts Jesus standing at a door holding a lantern, knocking, awaiting an invitation to enter a cottage. The painting was inspired by the Bible passage: "*Behold, I stand at the door and knock. If anyone hears my voice and opens the door, I will come into him and eat with him, and he with me*"(Rev. 3:20). While gazing upon the painting, one discovers that there is no doorknob on the outer door where Jesus is standing. The rusty nails and hinges are overgrown with ivy and weeds, presumably because the door hasn't been opened in years or perhaps never opened.

The door, which can only be opened from within, symbolizes the human heart, a heart which Jesus patiently hopes to make his home. Hollman's rendering, is a reminder that we must freely choose to invite Jesus to be our life's center.

Sadly, I believe that we are living in a culture of excessive busyness and multitasking. It is a culture that makes it more difficult to hear the divine knock of our Lord who awaits our response.

The worldly attractions of the secular culture, including social media outlets, have become the door so many are gravitating toward, as they spend countless hours each day, desperately seeking approval and tallying up the number of likes they are receiving on Facebook, Instagram, and Twitter. Another portal, which an increasing number of people are stepping through, is one that leads to immediate gratification, vice, and addiction. Sadly, many are dealing with addictions to opioids and other drugs. Some are caught up in the destructive vices of gambling, alcohol, and pornography. Taking lyrics from Johnny Lee," many are "Looking for love (and fulfillment) in all the wrong places."

Living through the current pandemic has also made it difficult for many to hear the divine knock of God's love, comfort, consolation, and peace as they suffer with depression, loneliness, isolation, anxiety, and stress.

While on retreat a few years ago, I recall walking into the chapel and seeing a sign above the chapel door of the retreat house, which read, *"Your cries have reached my ears"* (Deut. 3:9). The sign is a reminder to those who come through the door of the chapel that they will find the attentive listening heart of God waiting for them as they enter. I found that sign to be very comforting as I was about to begin my much-anticipated time of retreat prior to my priestly ordination. As I thought about those words, I realized how increasingly difficult it is becoming for many to hear that loving call of our Good Shepherd, calling us to enter through the door that will lead to communion with our loving God. Retreat houses, monasteries, and convents are beautiful, life-giving settings to develop a listening heart. The Oblates have a retreat house in Sarita, Texas, named *Lebshomea*, which in Hebrew means "listening heart." It is a place where people seek to come away to a quiet place and come into communion with our Lord.

A big part of my own vocation discernment, was my pilgrimage to Medjugorje in Sept 1989. For those unfamiliar with the miraculous events that have unfolded in Medjugorje, the following took place. On June 24, 1981, two young girls were walking in the hamlet of Bijakovici in the parish of Medjugorje when a woman holding an infant appeared high on a hill among the boulders and brambles of Mount Podbrdo. Instinctively, they knew it was the Virgin Mary, but they did not approach her. They and four other children felt called to return the next day, and our Blessed Mother drew them to her, effortlessly transporting them up the mountain, over boulders, and through thorny bushes.

The Blessed Virgin Mary introduced herself as the Queen of Peace. The children fell to their knees and began to pray. She prayed with them and promised to return the next day. Our Lady has regularly appeared in Medjugorje ever since, as have countless stories of conversion and miracles, making the story of Medjugorje one of the most fascinating in modern church history. The messages that our Blessed Mother has shared with the visionaries are messages of peace and love. Our Lady says God sent her to Medjugorje as an act of grace to remind us that God does exist, and He loves us.

She comes as the Queen of Peace to bring the world back to her Son. She has given us five "stones," or weapons, to combat evil and bring us closer to Jesus; they are prayer, fasting, scripture, Mass, the Eucharist, and the Sacrament of confession. Through her miraculous works and messages, she longs to open our hearts to God and help us to reorient our lives toward His Church and the Sacraments, which so many of us have moved away from.

During my own pilgrimage to this special place, there were no cell phones; the internet had not yet been invented, so I was cut off from the cacophony of the world's sounds. It was easy to settle into the mystery and deep peace of this beautiful hamlet. My ten days of prayer, mass, hiking the paths and climbing the mountain of the cross (Mt. Krizvac), enabled me to enter into a deep discernment concerning my vocation to religious life.

There were many other opportunities as well for me to be still and hear the inner voice of God speaking to my listening heart. Whether using the image of a listening heart or a divine knock, I realize how important it was to find those cherished moments of prayerful reflection—a time to come away to a quiet place and allow our Creator and Redeemer to speak to me.

Recalling the encounter that the prophet Elijah had with God on Mt. Horeb, it wasn't in an earthquake, a strong wind, or even in the fire that God spoke to Elijah. It was in a "gentle breeze." In that chapter, we read about the great prophet Elijah, who was being pursued by the evil queen Jezebel. She wanted to have him murdered because he was disrupting her plans. So Elijah flew into the desert. God sent an angel to strengthen him and send him on a long journey to Mt. Horeb. He spent the night in a cave on the mountainside. Fearful, confused, and depressed, Elijah prayed. Afterward, he went out to stand at the mouth of the cave, waiting for God's answer.

God was passing by.

At first, a mighty hurricane slammed into the mountain, shattering rocks and toppling trees. But God wasn't in the hurricane.

Then an earthquake shook the very foundations of the mountain, toppling cliffs and opening considerable fissures in the earth. But God wasn't in the earthquake either.

Then a massive fire swept over the side of the mountain, devouring everything in its path. But God wasn't in the fire.

Then, after all these expressions of power and intimidation, Elijah heard what sounded like a light murmuring sound, a whisper, a still small voice like a breeze."(1 Kings x:13–19)

That was the Lord who was respectfully, gently, politely sending his saving grace to his prophet who was in need. This is still how the Lord comes to us. He never forces his way into our lives. He is respectful of our freedom, desiring to form an everlasting, loving relationship with us. He always knocks first, awaiting our response.

In his visit to New York in 2008, Pope Benedict XVI pointed out:

> Have we perhaps lost something of the art of listening. Do you leave space to hear God's whisper, calling you forth into goodness. Friends, do not be afraid of silence of stillness, listen to God, adore him in the Eucharist. Let his word shape your journey.

I pray that all people especially those who are suffering, whether it be physically, emotionally, or spiritually, will one day hear the divine knock and respond to the one who created them out of love and wants nothing less than to offer them unconditional love, comfort, and healing. May they and all of us learn the language of silence in which we will hear the God who tells us, "Be still and know that I am God"(Ps. 46).

Sr. Joyce Rupp captures it well.

> Each of us needs an opportunity to be alone, and silent, to find space in the day of the week, to reflect and to listen to the voice of God that speaks deep within us.

> Our search for God is only our response to [God's] search for us. [God] knocks at our door, but for many people, their lives are too preoccupied for them to be able

> to hear. Let this day be one of a renewed
> desire to open the door of your heart.

I am very blessed indeed to have been able to hear the divine knock, which led to an amazing life as a priest. Still, I realized it isn't only about hearing a divine knock or learning the language of silence by developing a listening heart that is necessary to live a blessed life; it is also essential to have faith, trust, and courage to be able to open the door, taking that first step and beginning one's journey.

In the highly acclaimed film "*Lord of the Rings*": *The Fellowship of the Ring*," two hobbits, Frodo Baggins and his best friend Sam, are about to leave the comfort of their home in the shire and embark on a journey that will be filled with adventure, danger, joy, and life-giving friendships with the many characters they will encounter, including humans, elves, dwarfs, and even a wizard named Gandalf! Before embarking on their adventure, Sam turns to Frodo, saying, "It's a dangerous business, Frodo, going out your door. You step onto the road, and if you don't keep your feet, there's no knowing where you might be swept off to" (J.R.R. Tolkien).

For many of us, that first step of our journey, doesn't require stepping through some magical portal or negotiating some treacherous terrain. Instead, it requires stepping out of our comfort zones and stepping through the many doors of possibility. Again, stepping through any door that will lead to the unknown requires at least a little faith, trust, and courage, which many people can't seem to muster nowadays.

But as Joshua, one of the heroic figures of the Old Testament reminds us, *"Be strong and courageous…your God is with you wherever you go"* (Josh. 1:9).

> *Prayer: "O God, make the door of this house wide enough to receive all who need human love and fellowship, narrow enough to shut out all envy, pride, and strife….God, make the door of this house the gateway to Thine eternal kingdom" (unknown.)*

Passages from Scripture

"So I say to you, Ask, and it will be given you; search, and you will find; knock, and the door will be opened for you"(Luke 1:19).

"I know your works. Behold, I have set before you an open door, which no one can shut. I know that you have but little power, and yet you have kept my word and have not denied my name" (Rev. 3:8).

"I am at the door. If anyone enters by me, he will be saved and will go in and out and find pasture" (John 10:9).

Chapter Three

Roads

"And I know that if I do this, you will lead me by the right road, though I may know nothing about it. Therefore, I will trust you always though I may seem to be lost and in the shadow of death. I will not fear, for you are ever with me, and you will never leave me to face my perils alone." (The Road Ahead Prayer, *Thomas Merton*)

Roads are interesting places to encounter people who can have a lasting effect on our lives. Many people travel roads for many different reasons. I read an account of the famous writer Robert Louis Stevenson, who spent the final years of his life writing in the Samoan Islands. Stevenson befriended the natives of that island and often helped meet their financial needs and concerns. One story I read involved Stevenson investing in a new road to replace a very rocky and precarious dirt path that was the only route for the natives to travel from their village to the ocean where many made their living. Upon completion of the new road, the daily journey was made much easier to travel. The villagers thanked Stevenson for his generous gift and named the new pathway "The Road of a Loving Heart."

Recall how often it was on the road that many people's lives were transformed after encountering Jesus as he made his way from Galilee to Jerusalem. That road could also be named "The Road of a Loving Heart." Recall the encounter between Jesus and a blind man that took place on the way to Jericho:

> *Then they came to Jericho. As Jesus and his disciples, together with a large crowd, were leaving the city, a blind man, Bartimaeus (which means "son of Timaeus"), was sitting by the roadside begging. When he heard that it was Jesus of Nazareth, he began to shout, "Jesus, Son of David, have mercy on me!"*
>
> *Many rebuked him and told him to be quiet, but he shouted all the more, "Son of David, have mercy on me!"*
>
> *Jesus stopped and said, "Call him."*
>
> *So they called the blind man, "Cheer up! On your feet! He's calling you." Throwing his cloak aside, he jumped to his feet and came to Jesus.*

> *"What do you want me to do for you?" Jesus asked him.*
>
> *The blind man said, "Rabbi, I want to see."*
>
> *"Go," said Jesus, "your faith has healed you." Immediately he received his sight and followed Jesus along the road.* (Mark 10:46–59)

Another memorable encounter took place when two men encountered Jesus on the road to Emmaus:

> *When he was at the table with them, he took bread, gave thanks, broke it, and began to give it to them.*
>
> *Then their eyes were opened, and they recognized him, and he disappeared from their sight. They asked each other, "Were not our hearts burning within us while he talked with us on the road and opened the Scriptures to us?"* (Luke 24:31–34)

The Emmaus account is a beautiful image that captures the Mass that we celebrate as Catholics. The disciples recognize Jesus when he speaks (The liturgy of the Word) and during the breaking of the bread (The liturgy of the Eucharist). The Emmaus story also suggests that we are called to travel life's journey with others, sharing our faith, and supporting each other. Do we have the eyes of faith and hearts disposed to recognize Jesus in His living Word proclaimed in the Gospel and in the Eucharist offered at every Mass? Christ will be with us, opening our minds to the truth. Just as Jesus opened the minds and hearts of the disciples on the road to Emmaus, so he will do to all who believe. His promise remains, "I am with you, always!"

Jesus not only brought vast physical, emotional, and physical healing to many He encountered on the road. He also brought conversion of the heart (*metanoia*) to many people whose lives were transformed, including sinners and even tax collectors who were despised by the people of Israel and were looked upon as traitors to their people and loyal to the Romans who employed them.

Many Christians are familiar with two such tax collectors whose lives were transformed dramatically after an encounter with Jesus. Recall the scene that unfolds as Jesus traveled along the road through Jericho:

> *Jesus entered Jericho and was passing through. A man was there by the name of Zacchaeus; he was a chief tax collector and was wealthy. He wanted to see who Jesus was, but because he was short, he could not see over the crowd." So he ran ahead and climbed a sycamore-fig tree to see him since Jesus was coming that way.*

When Jesus reached the spot, he looked up and said to him, "Zacchaeus, come down immediately. I must stay at your house today." So he came down at once and welcomed him gladly.

All the people saw this and began to mutter, "He has gone to be the guest of a sinner." But Zacchaeus stood up and said to the Lord, "Look, Lord! Here and now I give half of my possessions to the poor, and if I have cheated anybody out of anything, I will pay back four times the amount."

Jesus said to him, "Today salvation has come to this house, because this man, too, is a son of Abraham. For the Son of Man came to seek and to save the lost."

(Luke 19:1–10)

Another well-known story involving a tax collector is the calling of Matthew, who would soon become one of Jesus' apostles.

As Jesus went on from there, he saw a man named Matthew sitting at the tax collector's booth.

> *"Follow me," he told him, and Matthew got up and followed him. While Jesus was having dinner at Matthew's house, many tax collectors and sinners came and ate with him and his disciples. When the Pharisees saw this, they asked his disciples, "Why does your teacher eat with tax collectors and sinners?"*
>
> *On hearing this, Jesus said, "It is not healthy who need a doctor, but the sick. But go and learn what this means: 'I desire mercy, not sacrifice.' I have not come to call the righteous but sinners." (Matt. 9:97–13)*

Perhaps the most memorable encounter that a person had on a road was the remarkable one that took place on the road to Damascus. An encounter that led a man from persecuting Christians to becoming the most significant missionary and evangelist in the history of the church. Of course, I'm referring to the encounter between Saul and Jesus:

> *Meanwhile, Saul was still breathing out murderous threats against the Lord's disciples. He went to the high priest and asked him for letters to the synagogues in Damascus, so that if he found any there who belonged to the Way, whether men or women, he might*

take them as prisoners to Jerusalem. As he neared Damascus on his journey, suddenly a light from heaven flashed around him. He fell to the ground and heard a voice say to him, "Saul, Saul, why do you persecute me?"

"Who are you, Lord?" Saul asked.

"I am Jesus, whom you are persecuting," he replied. "Now, get up and go into the city, and you will be told what you must do."

The men traveling with Saul stood there speechless; they heard the sound but did not see anyone. Saul got up from the ground, but when he opened his eyes, he could see nothing. So they led him by the hand into Damascus. For three days he was blind and did not eat or drink anything.

In Damascus, there was a disciple named Ananias. The Lord called to him in a vision, "Ananias!"

"Yes, Lord," he answered.

The Lord told him, "Go to the house of Judas on Straight Street and ask for a man from

Tarsus named Saul, for he is praying. In a vision, he has seen a man named Ananias come and place his hands on him to restore his sight."

"Lord," Ananias answered, "I have heard many reports about this man and all the harm he has done to your holy people in Jerusalem. And he has come here with authority from the chief priests to arrest all who call on your name."

But the Lord said to Ananias, "Go! This man is my chosen instrument to proclaim my name to the Gentiles and their kings and the people of Israel. I will show him how much he must suffer for my name."

Then Ananias went to the house and entered it. Placing his hands on Saul, he said, "Brother Saul, the Lord—Jesus, who appeared to you on the road as you were coming here—has sent me so that you may see again and be filled with the Holy Spirit." Immediately, something like scales fell from Saul's eyes, and he could see again. He got up and was baptized, and after taking some food, he regained his strength. (Acts 9:1–19)

So what is your story? How have you encountered Jesus along your road or path in life? How has He changed you? Who do you want to tell about it? After encountering Jesus, are we excited, like the Samaritan woman, running into town eager to share her experience with others? Many of the Samaritans from that town believed in Jesus because of the woman's testimony:

> *"He told me everything I ever did." So when the Samaritans came to him, they urged him to stay with them, and he stayed two days. And because of his words, many more became believers.*
>
> *They said to the woman, "We no longer believe just because of what you said; now we have heard for ourselves, and we know that this man is the Savior of the world."*(- John 4:39–42)

Through meditating on this passage, you can open your heart so that the Holy Spirit can refill it with God's love. Like the Samaritan woman, let us also open our hearts to listen trustingly to God's Word in order to encounter Jesus who reveals his love to us and tells us: *"I who speak to you am he, the Messiah, your Savior."*

All of these fantastic encounters with the divine one took place on different roads and paths, in different cities, towns, and villages. As another notable wisdom figure of our time wrote, *"People take different roads seeking fulfillment and happiness. Just because they're not on your road doesn't mean they've gotten lost" (The Dalai Lama)*

Prayer: "May the road rise to meet you. May the wind always be at your back. May the sun shine warm upon your face, and rains fall soft upon your fields" (Traditional Irish Blessing).

Scripture verses for meditation

> *"Watch the path of your feet*
> *And all your ways will be established"*
> *(Prov. 4:26)*

> *"Your word is a lamp to my feet And a light to my path" (Ps. 119).*

> *"He restores my soul;*
> *He guides me in the paths of righteousness*
> *For His name's sake" (Ps. 23:xx).*

Chapter Four

Feet

*"Christ has no body but yours,
No hands, no feet on earth but yours,
Yours are the eyes with which he looks
Compassion on this world,
Yours are the feet with which he walks
to do good"
(St. Teresa of Avila)*

We don't often think of our feet very often, yet we wouldn't have much of a journey without them. One mother I know gave the classic definition of the foot:
"A device used for finding LEGO's in the dark!" The master artist Leonardo Da Vinci described the foot as "A masterpiece of engineering and a work of art." After years of biking, hiking, and participating in all manner of sports, my dogs are barking, as the old adage goes! Everything from blisters, cuts, bruises, and bone spurs have assaulted my feet over the years of my journey. Monthly visits to the health club massage therapist, followed by a visit to the whirlpool, have been a tremendous blessing for my overworked and under-appreciated feet.

I imagine Jesus must have had some days where he couldn't wait to slip off his sandals after walking the miles of unpaved, rocky roads and traversing the hills and mountains mentioned in the Gospels. As he made his way from Galilee to Jerusalem, Jesus would climb mountains where he will deliver His Sermon on the Mount, feed the multitudes, undergo a transfiguration, and suffer a night of agony in a garden. Having walked some of those same roads and negotiated those mountains while visiting the holy land, My feet were ready for a good soak!

I remember visiting a retreat house in California where the chapel walls are decorated with a very unique and moving sculpture of the "Stations of the Cross." Each station was a bronze of the feet of Jesus as he walked the "Via Dolorosa" (The Way of Suffering). The sculptor of this unusual and creative depiction was able to capture the Lords' pain, suffering, and the heavy burden of the cross in His bare feet in such a unique way. I found the most moving station to be the fourth station where one notices two sets of feet touching. The feet are those of Jesus and His Blessed Mother Mary meeting along the way.

Great Artists and sculptors have been given such an amazing gift to be able to capture such emotion, sadness, joy, and other emotions in a person's eyes and face, hands, and yes, even feet. In the famous oil on canvas, *Return of the Prodigal Son*, Rembrandt Harmensz Van Rijn created what many consider his most exceptional work. The famous scene hangs in the State Hermitage Museum in

St. Petersburg's Russia. I first learned about this masterpiece after reading Henri Nouwen's excellent book *The Return of the Prodigal Son*. In a chapter focusing on the younger son returning to his father after squandering his share of his inheritance, Nouwen describes the moving scene in the following way:

Rembrandt leaves little doubt about the prodigal sons condition. His head is shaven...The head is that of a prisoner whose name has been replaced by a number. When a man's hair is shaved off, whether in prison or the army, in a hazing ritual or a concentration camp, he is robbed of one of the marks of his individuality. The clothes Rembrandt gives him are underclothes, barely covering his emaciated body. The father and the older brother observing the scene wear full red cloaks, giving them status and dignity. The kneeling son has no cloak.

The soles of the prodigal son's feet tell the story of a long and humiliating journey. The left foot, slipped out of its worn sandal, is scarred. The right foot, only partially covered by a broken sandal, also speaks of suffering and misery. This is a man dispossessed of everything. The original painting is eight feet in height and six feet in width. Although I have not made the journey to St. Petersburg to get up close and personal with the great work, I do have a print of it that I like to display during homilies and while directing Lenten retreats.

Upon an Untrodden Path

On the steps of the Basilica di Sant'Agostino in Rome, Italy, a stone's throw from Piazza Navona, a painting by the famous artist Caravaggio hangs. The painting is entitled *Madonna di Loreto*, (Madonna of the Pilgrims) and hangs above an altar in a narrow chapel. The painting depicts a poor elderly couple kneeling before Mary and the infant Jesus. They have walking sticks, indicating that they have made a journey to pay homage to the Madonna and child who look down on them with eyes of compassion and listening to their prayers and petitions. The story behind the painting is that it stirred a lot of negative criticism and controversy when it was first unveiled. The canvas was placed at eye level of the viewer, above an altar. When you look at it, one can see the faces of Jesus and Mary, but the elderly couple have their backs to the viewer. Those who approach the altar find themselves eye level with the grimy, weather-beaten soles of the old man in the painting who is barefoot.

Caravaggio, who was known to hire many of the poor street people as models for his paintings, often offended critics who frowned on the practice. Many felt it was irreverent to have a pair of filthy feet staring back at them as they approached the scene. On top of that, many thought it was disrespectful to have the painting hanging above the sacred altar. Over the centuries, millions of pilgrims, including me, have seen the painting. When I heard about the controversy, I thought how some must have forgotten about the humble beginnings of Jesus being born in a manger (feeding trough) and, in a great act of humility, would one day wash the feet of His apostles.

I recently read a story about another famous pair of feet that belonged to a recently canonized saint who spent most of her life on the impoverished streets of Calcutta India. A few years before Mother Theresa died, a Catholic monk named Shane Claiborne, who is part of Philadelphia's "The Simple Way" movement, had the opportunity to work and worship with the Missionaries of Charity in Calcutta. Brother Shane would join Mother Teresa and the sisters for prayer each day. He learned that all the sisters removed their sandals before entering the chapel and kneeled in prayer, as is the cultural practice for people in India and throughout much of Asia. On one occasion, Brother Shane was kneeling behind Mother Teresa, and was stunned to see that when Mother Teresa's feet were unshod, they were so gnarled and twisted they appeared to be crippled and deformed by some disease or deformity. After prayer, Shane asked one sister, "What disease caused Mother's feet to look like that."

"Oh, it's not a disease," the sister replied, "it's just that when the community receives a new donation of shoes, Mother always has everyone else choose first. She only wears whatever shoes are left over."

A lifetime of wearing mismatched, undersized, broken-out, crumpled-up shoes had transformed Mother Teresa's own feet into incompatible, undersized, broken, and crumpled appendages. Mother Teresa's feet reflected her dedication, her complete submersion of self in mission, in witness for Jesus, and love for her neighbor. The visible signs of a life of complete dedication was carried out on bruised, calloused feet. I wish I could present feet like that to our Lord after a life of serving others.

Prayer: "O Lord my God, help me to trust You with my decisions and my future. Let me lean on You with all my heart instead of relying on my own imperfect understanding.

Give me clear guidance in my life, Lord. As I submit myself to You, I know that You will direct my paths, and I can have confidence that Your direction is always the best way to go. Hear my prayer, Father. Through Jesus Christ, our Lord, Amen."

Scripture passages for meditation

"Your word is a lamp to my feet and a light to my path" (Ps. 119:105)

"And make straight paths for your feet, so that what is lame may not be put out of joint but rather be healed" (Heb. 12:13).

"Ponder the path of your feet; then all your ways will be sure" (Prov. 4:26).

"You put my feet in the stocks and watch all my paths; you set a limit for the soles of my feet" (Job 13 27).

Chapter Five

Suffering Along the Journey

"The world breaks everyone, and afterward, many are strong at the broken places" (*A Farewell to Arms*, Ernest Hemingway)

I believe many of us can identify with that statement. The truth is that no one is spared suffering in this life. How one views suffering will determine whether one will grow stronger or weaker physically, emotionally, and spiritually as we face the trials and tribulations that suffering will bring upon us. One of my dear friends Alice who is a parishioner at St. Mary's, is one of the most selfless people I have met in quite a long time. Alice runs a fabric business in San Antonio. In addition to supplying fabrics to people who love to sew and quilt, Alice is a very gifted quilter.

She has made many quilts for her family, friends, parishioners, and people she has never even met, including my mother and three sisters. My sister Diane who was born on January 8 shares a birthday with the king of rock and roll—Elvis Presley. Alice presented me with a quilt with images of Elvis from the movie *Jail House Rock*.

Diane keeps that quilt by the fireplace of her home and wraps it around herself on those chilly New York evenings.

Many of those quilts have provided joy, comfort, consolation and a feeling of security for people celebrating a birthday or anniversary, to snuggle in on Christmas morning and many other occasions. Sometimes the quilt is made in the form of a friendship quilt with inscriptions sewn in. Among the most meaningful quilts that Alice creates, are those for a grieving family. Some of the quilts even contain bits of clothing that had belonged to the lost loved one. I told Alice that the very act of working on such a quilt and presenting it to a grieving loved one was like the image of Jesus pulling a person into the crossing of His arm, close to His Sacred Heart. No wonder why people wrap those quilts around themselves when they receive one . Numerous quilts were made in the wake of the tragedy of September 11, 2001, demonstrating that quilting in the face of shock and sorrow is a tremendous comfort!

As a parish priest, one of the many responsibilities I have include visiting local hospitals, nursing homes, hospice facilities, prisons, and homeless shelters. These visits are a constant reminder that suffering is a part of everyone's journey. I have tried to impart upon the people I visit, that suffering is not some meaningless form of pain that only brings with it despair, depression, hopelessness, and fear. Understanding suffering as having redemptive value has given many people the strength to endure it.

Suffering Along the Journey

When the 1994 World Day of the Sick was celebrated at the Shrine of Our Lady of Czestochowa in Poland, Pope John Paul II reflected on the tribulations of suffering in this life as a sign of future glory. In this light, the Holy Father proclaimed that "Human suffering can, through God's grace and his great design of salvation, contribute to redemption. In the course of the same celebration, the Pope addressed the many pilgrims who were experiencing pain in its many forms, urging them to face their suffering without being discouraged and yielding to pessimism. The Holy Father called upon them to realize that their suffering when borne with the spirit of faith can be an instrument of redemption. The Holy Father continued:

Take the opportunity opened up by Christ to transform your situation into an expression of grace and love. Then your pain, too, will become salvific and contribute to completing the suffering of Christ for the benefit of his Body which is the Church.

As a priest, I realize that I have the responsibility to bring the message of redemptive suffering to those carrying a heavy cross. The anointing of the sick is one of the great sacraments that a priest brings to those who are suffering. The main scriptural foundation for the sacrament of the Anointing of the Sick is found in the Letter of James: "*Is any among you sick. Let him call for the elders of the church and let them pray over him, anointing him with oil in the name of the Lord*" (James 5:14).

This sacrament is not just for the benefit of the afflicted person; the whole Church benefits when suffering is offered up for him/her.

The Catechism describes this sacrament as an "ecclesial grace":

The sick who receive this sacrament, by freely uniting themselves to the passion and death of Christ, contribute to the good of the People of God.' By celebrating this sacrament the Church, in the communion of saints, intercedes for the benefit of the sick person, and he, for his part, though the grace of this sacrament, contributes to the sanctification of the Church and to the good of all men for whom the Church suffers and offers herself through Christ to God the Father. (CCC 1522)

For Christians, the Cross is not only the symbol of Christ's suffering, but it is also seen as an instrument of our redemption and salvation. The Cross brings Christians a profound understanding of why God allows suffering along our journey of faith. Through his suffering on the Cross, we believe that Jesus took our sins upon Himself for the salvation of the world. As stated in the Gospel, "*For God so loved the world, that he gave his only Son, that whoever believes in him should not perish but have eternal life*" (John 3:16). When Jesus began his public ministry, it was John the Baptist who pointed toward him and uttered the profound and prophetic words: "*Behold, the Lamb of God, who takes away the sin of the world!*" (John 1:29).

Jesus emphasizes that we cannot separate the cross from our role as disciples on the road toward salvation. In the Gospel of Matt, Jesus states emphatically: *"If anyone would come after me, let him deny himself and take up his cross and follow me. For whoever would save his life will lose it, but whoever loses his life for my sake will find it"* (Matt. 16:9). Dr. David Anderson, in his book *Triumph Through Trials,* states, "Trials are not optional; they are inevitable. Trials are a normal part of God's process of bringing us to glory." As the body of Christ, the Church, we are called to unite our suffering with that of our Savior.

In his letter to the Romans, Paul makes the connection between pain and our salvation. Paul writes: *"We are children of God, and if children, then heirs, heirs of God and fellow heirs with Christ—if we suffer with him so that we may also be glorified with him"* (Rom. 8:16–17). Paul continues: *"For I consider that the sufferings of this present time are not worthy of being compared with the glory that is to be revealed to us"* (Rom. 8:18). Paul doesn't deny that, as Christians, we will have to suffer in this world, as Jesus proclaimed. However he points out that the goal of our journey "eternal life" is well worth those sufferings. In Acts of the Apostles, Paul adds that it is *"through many tribulations, we must enter the kingdom of God"*

(Acts 14:22).

I often think of the many saints and martyrs who truly embraced the cross and lay down their lives in witness to the teachings of Christ and his church. St Maximilian Kolbe was one such martyr. For those of who may not be familiar with his story. St. Maximilian was a Polish

Franciscan priest, arrested by the Gestapo during World War II. After his arrest, Fr. Maximilian was sent to the concentration camp at Auschwitz, where he was treated with brutality because he was a Catholic priest.

Many have heard of the famous incident that took place at the camp, when a fellow prisoner, Franciszek Gajowniczek, a Polish army sergeant, who was married with children, was condemned by the camp commander to be executed along with several other POWs. Fr. Maximilian offered to take the place of Gajowniczek, knowing that it would mean certain death. His offer was accepted, and he died with the other condemned prisoners in a starvation bunker. A fellow prisoner who survived the camp witnessed on behalf of Fr. Maximilian, stating the following:

"Each time I saw Father Kolbe in the courtyard, I felt within myself an extraordinary effusion of his goodness. Although he wore the same ragged clothes as the rest of us, with the same tin can hanging from his belt, one forgot this wretched exterior and was conscious only of the charm of his inspired countenance and his radiant holiness."

Years ago, I read an account of another amazing person of courage. Toward the end of his life, Archbishop Fulton J. Sheen was asked who was the greatest influence on his life. To many people's surprise, he told the journalist that it was a ten-year-old girl named Li, the Eucharistic martyr of China.

Suffering Along the Journey

Li lived at the time of one of the darkest periods in China's history. right after Mao Zedong completed his communist takeover of China. God was no longer allowed to be mentioned, and people who practiced their Christian belief in Him were either imprisoned, tortured, or killed by the ruling political class who were all communists. In the morning of the day that would change little Li's life, Li and her fellow students were diligently reciting their prayers, learning their lessons, and enjoying the warm, friendly confines of their classroom. Their teacher, Sr. Euphrasia, had joyfully witnessed the many of the children receive their first Holy Communion two months earlier.. Like their ancestors before them, the children knew how important rice was in their daily diet. When little Li was taught the Lord's prayer, ten-year-old Li asked Sr. Euphrasia why Jesus didn't say, "Give us this day our daily rice." Sister Euphrasia smiled knowing that bread was an unfamiliar meal for the children. She explained that we need rice for the body, but that in asking for daily bread, we are really asking for Holy Communion. This is the food for the soul, and this bread is the "Bread of Life." In May 1953, when Li made her First Communion, she had asked Jesus in her heart and prayed, "Always give me that daily bread so that my soul can live and be healthy!" From that day on, Li received Holy Communion every day.

She would never forget the day the communist soldiers burst through the classroom room and screamed at the children, demanding that they hand over all their religious articles of faith, including rosaries, crosses, medals, scapulars, and holy cards. The terrified children gave up their carefully hand-painted pictures of Jesus, Mary, and the Saints. Then in a fit of rage, the commanding officer pulled the Crucifix off the wall, threw it down on the ground, and trampled on it, screaming: "The New China will not tolerate these grotesque superstitions!" Little Li, who loved her picture of the Good Shepherd so much, attempted to hide it in her blouse. It was the special image given to her for her First Holy Communion. A soldier noticed and pulled it from her blouse, tearing it up and throwing it to the floor. The soldier then slapped little Li across the face, sending her crashing to the floor.

That same day, the police made a sweep of the village, corralling all its citizens and funneling them into the village Church. Once gathered, the inspector ridiculed the villagers' beliefs, telling them that they were tricked into believing that God is present in the tabernacle. The people watched with disbelief, as the commander ordered the soldiers to fire at the tabernacle. After the Tabernacle was damaged irreparably by the hail of bullets, the commander grabbed the ciborium, containing the Body, Blood, Soul, and Divinity of Jesus and threw all the Sacred Hosts onto the tile floor. Stunned, the faithful turned their gaze away from this awful man and the sacrilegious act he had just carried out, all the time trying to hold back their tears. Little Li froze in horror. Her innocent and righteous little heart bled for the Sacred Hosts strewn all over the ground. *Isn't anyone going to help Jesus?"* she wondered in amazement.

The commander continued his tirade of rage and insults, as the villagers and little Li wept silently. "Now get out!" the inspector yelled. "And woe to anyone who returns to this den of superstition! He'll answer to me!" Before they left, the soldiers locked Fr. Luke the pastor of the church, in the coal bunker near the sacristy, leaving him to die. A small opening in the bunker, helped Fr. Luke to see through to the sanctuary where the Blessed Sacrament lay strewn on the floor. The church quickly emptied.

Through the little opening Fr. Luke would notice as the dawn broke the next morning, the arrival of little Li, who very quietly entered the Church. Slowly, she made her way into the sanctuary. Fr. Luke could not call out to little Li, fearing that it might draw attention from the soldiers who were not far from the church. Unable to communicate with her, Fr. Luke could only watch and pray for her safety. He observed as the little girl bowed for a moment and adored the Blessed Sacrament laying on the floor.

Little Li stayed with Jesus in adoration for one whole hour, knowing that she was supposed to prepare her heart before receiving Him. Her hands joined together, she whispered a prayer to her Jesus who was so mistreated and abandoned. Father Luke never took his eyes off the young girl, and he continued to observe her as she lowered herself down on her knees, bent over, and with her tongue, took up one of the Hosts. She then remained there on her knees, eyes closed and in deep joy at having received her Lord Jesus Christ. Father Luke was moved to tears as watched this ten-year-old girl exhibit such faith, trust, and courage. Li quietly stood up left the Church unnoticed.

Meanwhile, the Communists searched the entire village to rid it of any and all Christian images. As the villagers stayed in their homes, living in fear of persecution and death, little Li slipped away from her sleeping family early each morning to adore our Lord for one hour and consume the Blessed Sacrament with love and reverence. Father Luke, concerned for her safety, couldn't understand why she didn't take more than one. He knew exactly how many Hosts had been in the ciborium: there were thirty-two of them, and surely she would be seen if she snuck into the church for thirty two days. But, Li didn't do that, as Sister had taught the children they could have only one Host per day, and they were never to touch it except with the tongue. The little girl kept to all she had been taught because she knew just how precious the Host was: it was Jesus Himself really and truly present in it.

Father Luke was relieved when the last day came around. This day, Li would adore Jesus and consume the last of His Sacred Body. At dawn, Li entered the church as usual and drew near to the altar. She knelt to the ground to pray very close to Jesus in the Sacred Host. Father Luke had to stifle a cry when a soldier suddenly appeared at the church door and aimed his gun at her. A single shot was heard, followed by a snicker. The child immediately collapsed. Father Luke thought she was dead, but no! Grief stricken, he watched her struggle to crawl over to where the Host was, and could hardly believe his eyes when, in obvious pain, she put her tongue over the Sacred Host to receive her Jesus for the last time. She then drew her last breath and died a true martyr's death.

For a moment, the soldier simply looked as if trying to make sense of the terrible thing he just did. Then, he turned and rushed out of the church, but not before releasing Father Luke, telling him he was free to go. Without any hesitation, Fr. Luke rushed to the sanctuary to see the lifeless body of the little girl. As he knelt beside her, Fr. Luke sobbed heavily! After a few moments, he gathered up little Li and quickly took her to the church cemetery nearby. Father Luke just had enough time to give little

Li a decent burial before the soldiers would return. As he left the cemetery and walked along the road, a man approached and invited him into his car. He dropped him off at the border. The priest escaped death and was now free, and that is the very reason we know about the story of this beautiful young Chinese girl martyr today.

Little Li was dead, but not before she had ensured that the Eucharist would not be further desecrated. Though gone from this world, her memory still lives on as it did in the person of Archbishop Sheen, and in the countless millions of people worldwide that he, through her story, was encouraged to pray a holy hour as often as possible before the Blessed Sacrament. Archbishop Fulton Sheen knew that Little Li understood perfectly that he Blessed Sacrament is Jesus, Light of the world and the joy of all hearts. O how He longs for people to treat Him with respect and to pay due reverence to Him in the tabernacle when we go into our churches.

Prayer: "Behold me, my beloved Jesus, weighed down under the burden of my trials and sufferings, I cast myself at Your feet, that You may renew my strength and my courage, while I rest here in Your Presence. Permit me to lay down my cross in Your Sacred Heart, for only Your infinite goodness can sustain me; only Your love can help me bear my cross; only Your powerful hand can lighten its weight. O divine King, Jesus, whose heart is so compassionate to the afflicted, I wish to live in You and suffer and die in You. During my life, be to me my model and my support. At the hour of my death, be my hope and my refuge. Amen."

Scripture for meditation

> *"Praise be to the God and Father of our Lord Jesus Christ, the Father of compassion and the God of all comfort, who comforts us in all our troubles so that we can comfort those in any trouble with the comfort we ourselves receive from God." (2 Cor.1:3)*

> *"Very truly I tell you, you will weep and mourn while the world rejoices. You will grieve, but your grief will turn to joy" (John 16:20).*

> *"As a mother comforts her child, so will I comfort you; and you will be comforted over Jerusalem" (Isa. 66:13).*

Chapter Six

Detours Along the Journey

"When you come to a fork in the road, take it" (Yogi Berra).

As I was looking for various themes revolving around life's journey, I thought about how many detours we encounter along our travels, detours that often take us in directions we hadn't planned on or expected. Although we don't often think of detours in a positive light, detours along our journey can open up an entirely new world of possibilities for us. Many people will embark with laser-like focus on what they believe to be their purpose in life, only to find that journey upended as we suddenly find ourselves facing a dead-end or a detour. At first, these obstacles can be a source of discouragement, anxiety, anger, and stress. Detours can even lead to disastrous consequences, as we have seen throughout history. One example that I found both fascinating and tragic, involves the assassination of Archduke Ferdinand in Sarajevo in 1914 that led to the First World War.

Apparently, the driver of Archduke Ferdinand spoke only Czech and did not understand the orders given by

German security officers to follow a particular road that was considered safe. The driver took a detour that was quicker but much more dangerous! Archduke Ferdinand would fall victim to an assassin's bullet. One historian would write that "Seventeen million people would eventually die because one man took a wrong turn."

Detours can also yield amazing and life-giving fruit. Many are familiar with the discovery of the "Dead Sea Scrolls" which were found quite a by accident, when in 1946, a couple of Bedouin teenagers were tending their goats and sheep near the ancient settlement of Qumran, located on the northwest shore of the Dead Sea in what is now known as the West Bank.

One of the young shepherds threw a stone into a cave opening on the side of a cliff face. The shepherd heard the rock shattering something that sounded like glass. The shepherds entered the cave and found a collection of large clay jars, seven of which contained leather and papyrus scrolls. An antiquities dealer bought the cache, which ultimately ended up in the hands of various scholars who estimated that the texts were upwards of 2,000 years old.

The word of the discovery got out, and Bedouin treasure hunters and archaeologists unearthed tens of thousands of additional scroll fragments from ten nearby caves; together, they make up between 800 and 900 manuscripts known as the "Dead Sea Scrolls." Detours in one's life may seem at first to be a source of frustration, inconvenience, and even stress, yet very often these detours can be a blessing in disguise.

The detours in my own life have been a wonderful source of growth as they have challenged me to go beyond my comfort zone and explore the unfamiliar, the unknown, and the mysterious. One movie that I like to use as an illustration of detours along the journey, is the 1995 hit, *Mr. Holland's Opus*. For those of you unfamiliar with the story, it revolves man named Glen Holland, who dreams of creating a symphony—a grand opus that will ensure that his life will not be a wasted one. Unlike other great composers like Mozart and Beethoven, who were well paid to compose and create full time, Glen has to pay the bills for himself, his wife Iris, and his son Cole who was born deaf. Eventually, Glen Holland takes a job teaching music in a Portland high school, never realizing that he will have fewer and fewer opportunities to work on his great opus. As the years pass, more and more detours appear along Mr. Holland's Journey, pulling him further and further away from finishing his great symphony.

In addition to teaching music, Mr. Holland must supplement his income to support his family by teaching drivers education to the students after school. The years pass by, and we see a much-older Glen Holland cleaning out his desk after receiving the sad news that the music program has been cut over budget concerns. He believes that his life has not added up to very much as he walks downtrodden toward the school exit, his wife and son in tow, carrying his personal effects. Suddenly the sound of music coming from the school auditorium catches their attention. The three open the auditorium door where Mr. Holland and his family are greeted with thunderous applause and cheers from the many students and faculty both past and present whose lives have been touched by Mr. Holland over the years. One former student who is now the governor of the state takes the stage and reminds Mr. Holland of just what an extraordinary influence he has been in the lives of many of his students. In a moving, final scene, The governor states the following, "Mr. Holland had a profound influence on my life, and on a lot of lives I know, and yet I get the feeling that he considers a great part of his own life misspent. Rumor has it, he was always working on this symphony of his, and this was going to make him famous, rich, probably both.

But Mr. Holland isn't rich, and he isn't famous, at least not outside of our little town. So it might be easy for him to think of himself as a failure. And he would be wrong because I think he's achieved a success far beyond riches and fame. Look around you. There is not a life in this room that you have not touched, and each one of us is a better person because of you! We are your symphony, Mr. Holland. We are the melodies and the notes of your opus. And we are the music of your life!"

As we journey through life, we often find that our journey can be uprooted, detoured, and set spinning off course. As one comedian wrote, "If you want to make

God laugh, tell him your plans!" Like Mr. Holland, I felt sure that I was on the right path throughout my life, from childhood hopes and dreams of playing in the major leagues to becoming a great warrior, as my brothers Bob and Joe and I acted out battles with our green army men and GI Joes in our backyard. As a teen, I felt sure that I would become a great drummer who would one day even rival the great Buddy Rich. I loved playing the drums and listening to the great drummers of jazz, big band, and rock, like Steve Gadd, Peter Erskine, and Neil Peart (RIP). My best friend in high school, Billy, was a very talented bass player. Billy and I lived, breathed, and slept music in high school. Billy's dad, Ed, was a great drummer in his own right, and when I told him how much I loved the sound, dexterity, and driving rhythms of the great drummers, he offered to teach me. I was thrilled and would spend the next eight years learning from my music mentor, Big Ed.

All the cash Billy and I managed to rake in from shoveling snow, delivering newspapers, busing tables, and discovering loose change between the cushions of our parent's couches went toward stereo equipment, replacing broken drumsticks and bass strings, and purchasing albums of our favorite bands. One year, my wonderful and very patient and loving parents, Bob and Teresa, would surprise me with my first drum kit, which will always be a great memory and remind me in the many ways that God has blessed me with the greatest of parents! Once Billy and I started jamming together, Billy on his Fender bass and me on my Ludwig drum kit, we were off and running on our quest to fulfill what I thought was the reason God had fashioned me in my mother's womb.

In addition to jamming to the legends of jazz, rock and fusion, we amassed a collection of albums that would make us the envy of our high school. Billy and I were the two favorite customers at Straub Music in Plainview, New York, where we both grew up. It was a music store run by a free-spirited hippie couple named Jim and Roxy.

Presently, Bill is a studio musician playing his bass and living his dream in Colorado with his wife and children. My own journey, however, would have a few more detours ahead. To paraphrase St. Agustine, I was living with a restless heart that was waiting to find its true home. Looking at the scriptures, I realize that hitting a detour is an all too common theme for many of God's children. I have come to realize that I was in good company with a few fishermen who were detoured and taken on a journey that would change their lives forever. Recall the following?

> *As Jesus was walking beside the Sea of Galilee, he saw two brothers, Simon called Peter and his brother Andrew. They were casting a net into the sea, for they were fishermen.*
>
> *"Come, follow me," Jesus said, "and I will make you fishers of men." At once, they left their nets and followed him."*

> *Going on from there, he saw two other brothers, James son of Zebedee and his brother John. They were in a boat with their father Zebedee, preparing their nets. Jesus called them, and immediately they left the boat and their father and followed him.* (Matt. 4:18–22)

Perhaps the most extraordinary story of a detour in the life of someone Christians have come to love and honor is the story of a young maiden who exhibited great faith, trust, and courage throughout her life, our Blessed Mother Mary:

> *In the sixth month of Elizabeth's pregnancy, God sent the angel Gabriel to Nazareth, a town in Galilee, to a virgin pledged to be married to a man named Joseph, a descendant of David. The virgin's name was Mary.*
>
> *The angel went to her and said, "Greetings, you who are highly favored! The Lord is with you."*
>
> *Mary was greatly troubled at his words and wondered what kind of greeting this might be. But the angel said to her, "Do not be afraid, Mary; you have found favor with God. You*

will conceive and give birth to a son, and you are to call him Jesus. He will be great and will be called the Son of the Highest.

"The Lord God will give him the throne of his father David, and he will reign over Jacob's descendants forever; his kingdom will never end."

"How will this be," Mary asked the angel, "since I am a virgin?"

The angel answered, "The Holy Spirit will come on you, and the power of the Highest will overshadow you. So the holy one to be born will be called[a] the Son of God. Even Elizabeth, your relative, is going to have a child in her old age, and she who was said to be unable to conceive is in her sixth month. For nothing will be impossible for God."

"I am the Lord's servant," Mary answered. "Let it be done according to your word." (Luke 1:26–38)

Mary's fiat will take her on a journey that will not only affect her own life but the lives of all Christians.

Mary's fiat will prepare the way for the long-awaited Messiah!

One thing I learned about detours over the years, is that we often don't see them coming, whether while driving on a highway or settling into our careers and vocations. They catch us off-guard, leaving us frustrated, confused, hopeful, and curious. We question why things had to happen this way. As I am writing this chapter of the book, I am sitting on the roof of the rectory here at my parish of St. Mary's, overlooking the river walk of San Antonio below. I am very blessed to be the pastor of such a wonderful parish with great people!

Presently, the city of San Antonio is in the midst of significant growth with several construction projects underway. From new hotel and restaurant projects in the downtown area, to road and highway extensions, detours and road closures have become a way of life here. As I was driving one morning and ran into a detour, it dawned on me that one way to look at a detour is that it often indicates that something is in the process of being improved soon. When God takes us on a detour, He is also in the process of improving us. He may be calling us to uproot the impurities in our hearts brought about through sin, as He invites us to the sacrament of reconciliation. God may be inviting us to step off the fast-paced highway of multitasking and our frenetic paced days and exhausting routines. We must realize that what may look like an inconvenient detour may be an invitation to come away to a quiet place where Jesus will speak to our hearts.

The ultimate temptation is to become discouraged, even angry at God, when He places a detour along our path, but take comfort in these words: *"You do not understand now what I am doing, but you will understand later on"* (John 13:7). God hopes that you and I will cooperate with his divine plan for us. This is how we become the people He created us to be.

Prayer:

> " Heavenly Father, thank You for these lessons on detours and how You use them to positively impact my life. Please open my eyes to see how You have done this in my past and even how You are presently doing this in the situations I face. I want to approach life's detours in a mature manner, so I don't cause additional delays. Increase my wisdom, patience, and insight so I can honor You in all of life's detours. In Jesus's name, Amen.

Scripture for meditation

> *"Jesus said to him, "I am the way, and the truth, and the life. No one comes to the Father except through me" (John 14:6).*

"For I am sure that neither death nor life, nor angels nor rulers, nor things present nor things to come, nor powers, nor height nor depth, nor anything else in all creation, will be able to separate us from the love of God in Christ Jesus our Lord."(Rom. 8:38–39)

"I will send my messenger ahead of you, who will prepare your way, a voice of one calling in the wilderness, Prepare the way for the Lord, make straight paths for him." (Mark 1:3)

Chapter Seven

Lighting the Way

"A single sunbeam is enough to drive away many shadows" (**St. Francis of Assisi**).

Some of you might recall the story of a battleship that was on a training exercise at sea in bad weather. The captain was on the bridge. It was foggy. Just after dark, the lookout spotted a light on the starboard side. The captain asked if it was steady or moving. The lookout replied the light was steady, meaning they were on a direct collision course with the other ship!

The captain ordered the lookout signal to the other boat: "Change course 20 degrees. We are on a collision course."

The signal came back '" Advisable for you to change course."

The captain signaled, "'I am a captain. Change course 20 degrees."

"You had better change course 20 degrees!" came the reply.

The captain was furious! He sent back, "I am a battleship. Change course!"

Back came the signal, "I am a lighthouse. Your call."

Lighthouses have always been a great source of direction, guidance, and safety during the journeys of many people for centuries. Just think of how many lives were saved because of these structures lighting the way to ports of safety throughout the world. The ancient tower of Hercules is the oldest standing lighthouse remaining in the world. Built in Galicia, Spain, around the second century by the Romans, it was initially known as the *Farum Brigantium*

or "Brigantia Lighthouse." According to myth, it also marks the resting place of one of Hercules' greatest conquests. Amazingly, it is still a functioning lighthouse and continues guiding ships that have made journeys of thousands of miles at sea into its safe harbor. That is the noble purpose of a lighthouse, to light the way and to warn of danger. Its light is meant for all.

In the Gospel of John, Jesus proclaims that he is the "Light of the World" who guides us with his unconditional love, mercy, and forgiveness as we journey through life. The image of light has always been a life-giving one, bringing to mind thoughts of warmth, safety, comfort, and security. As the light of the world, Jesus is the one whose presence will always dispel the darkness of sin, death, and evil! Jesus pierces the darkness of sin, corruption, and death and conquers it. Jesus is *"The light that shines in the darkness, and the darkness has not overcome it"* (John 1:5).

Lighting the Way

In the Judeo/Christian tradition, the image of light is a familiar one. The very beginning of the journey of faith for most Christians begins when they receive the sacrament of baptism. One of the gifts we receive during baptism is a candle that is lit from the paschal candle that represents the light of Jesus Christ. The newly baptized receives the candle with the words, "Receive the light of Christ," which is pronounced by a priest or deacon. The light of Christ has now been transmitted to him/her through baptism. Every Easter Vigil, we bless and light the Paschal (Easter) candle. Everyone attending the Vigil Mass will once again light a candle from the Paschal candle to witness that the light of Christ will continue to spread throughout the world through those of us who belong to Him.

Years ago, I met a wonderful priest named Fr. Raj who was born and raised in a poor village in central India, a place where many of the people residing in the towns and villages are living at or below the poverty line. Most of the churches in his town and the neighboring villages have no electricity or running water. Fr. Raj explained to me that one church had little natural light penetrating the interior from the outside, which made it difficult for the people to read their hymnals and prayer books. A young, creative priest was eventually assigned to the church, and among the first of the many issues he addressed at the church was its poor lighting. He ultimately came up with a brilliant idea.

He was able to secure several donations from more affluent Catholics in a nearby city, and with the funds, he had a large iron chandelier with a corkscrew-like design made.

Upon its completion, he purchased one oil lantern for each family of the parish. The idea was that as each family entered to church for mass, they would place their lantern on the iron fixture, which would slowly dispel the darkness of the church and bring much-needed light within. After a while, the people began to feel more and more connected as a parish family as they realized that all their lanterns together would illuminate the church beautifully. People also started to check up on their neighbors more often if they saw a lantern missing from the chandelier.

This story gave me a new insight into the beautiful account of the "Transfiguration."

> *After six days, Jesus took with him Peter, James, and John, the brother of James, and led them up a high mountain by themselves. There he was transfigured before them. His face shone like the sun, and his clothes became as white as the light.*
>
> *Just then there appeared before them Moses and Elijah, talking with Jesus.*

Peter said to Jesus, "Lord, it is good for us to be here. If you wish, I will put up three shelters— one for you, one for Moses and one for Elijah."

While he was still speaking, a bright cloud covered them, and a voice from the cloud said, "This is my Son, whom I love; with him, I am well pleased. Listen to him!"

When the disciples heard this, they fell facedown to the ground, terrified. But Jesus came and touched them. "Get up," he said. "Don't be afraid." When they looked up, they saw no one except Jesus.

As they were coming down the mountain, Jesus instructed them, "Don't tell anyone what you have seen, until the Son of Man has been raised from the dead."

(Luke 9:28–36)

The Transfiguration was not only an incredible event that occurred on a mountain top, it is also an invitation to allow the divine light of Christ to shine through our humanity. If more Christians recognized this beautiful gift and allowed the light of Christ to shine through their human nature, we could bring those lights together, dispelling much of the darkness in the world we are living in.

The great Winston Churchill, Prime Minister of England during World War II, and the glue that held Britain together in the dark hours of that struggle recognized this. Churchill was not Catholic himself, but soon after the war had ended, he visited a Catholic convent of cloistered nuns to thank them for their prayers for the country. His experience deeply moved him. Before he left, he told the nuns that they and the other convents like theirs were like a "ring of bright lights on the shores of a black, burnt-out world." I believe that when Churchill visited that order of nuns, he witnessed a holy, transfigured group of women who had the divine light of Christ shining through their human nature.

> Prayer: "God, You send us to be lights in a dark world. With the power of Your Spirit and Your Word, we have the courage to confess our faith in Your Son, Jesus Christ, in whose name we pray. Amen" (Columban Fathers).

Scripture for meditation

"The light shines in the darkness, and the darkness has not overcome it" (John 1:5).

"I am the light of the world. Whoever follows me will never walk in darkness but will have the light of life."(John 8:12)

"The LORD is my light and my salvation—whom shall I fear. The LORD is the stronghold of my life—of whom shall I be afraid." (Ps. 27:1)

Chapter 8:

Food for the Journey

"Recognize in this bread what hung on the cross, and in this chalice what flowed from His side" (St. Augustine).

In his very well-researched and compelling book entitled, *Jesus and the Jewish Roots of the Eucharist*, Brant Pitre writes the following: " Remember that in the Old Testament, the people of Israel did not go straight from Egypt to the promised land. Their journey took years of wandering in the desert—forty years, to be exact (Num. 32:13). "Known by ancient Jews as the "wilderness wandering," this journey was a time of great trial and tribulation. During those years, Israel's fidelity to their God was tested over and over again. And during that time in the desert, God sustained them on a daily basis by giving them special food: the manna from heaven." This theme of food for the journey is present in both the Old Testament and New Testaments.

As I mentioned a few chapters ago, in J. R. R. Tolkien's masterwork, *The Lord of the Rings*, we are introduced to two hobbits, Frodo and Sam, who set out on a dangerous quest. At one point, they are given a special kind of bread by the elves called *lembas*. Lembas translates to "journey bread" and has the power to sustain a person for an entire day's journey after just one bite. Unlike the Lembas bread that will only satisfy one for a day, the Eucharist is our journey food. The divine nourishment that strengthens us in body and spirit.

In the Gospels, Jesus speaks of another kind of bread, "The Bread of Life"—His own body and blood in the Eucharist. But unlike *lembas,* it is not some fictitious, magical food. It is the body, blood, soul, and divinity of Jesus Himself. When we receive the Eucharist, we are receiving Jesus, not a symbol, but his real presence! This belief is supported in scripture where we read the profound proclamation spoken by Jesus.

> *Amen, Amen, I say to you unless you eat the flesh of the Son of Man and drink his blood, you do not have life within you. Whoever eats my flesh and drinks my blood has eternal life, and I will raise him on the last day. For my flesh is true food, and my blood is true drink.*
> (John: 6:53–54)

The liturgy of the Eucharist is the most sacred and revered part of the Holy Mass, in which we remember and recite the events that unfolded at the Last Supper.

When the hour came, Jesus and his apostles reclined at the table. And he said to them, "I have eagerly desired to eat this Passover with you before I suffer. I tell you, I will not eat it again until it finds fulfillment in the kingdom of God."

After taking the cup, he gave thanks and said, "Take this and divide it among you. For I tell you I will not drink again from the fruit of the vine until the kingdom of God comes."

And he took bread, gave thanks and broke it, and gave it to them, saying, "This is my body given for you; do this in remembrance of me."

In the same way, after the supper he took the cup, saying, "This cup is the new covenant in my blood, which is poured out for you."
(Luke 14–21)

Recalling these words of Jesus, the Catholic Church professes that, in the celebration of the Eucharist, the bread and wine offered on the altar become the body and blood of Jesus Christ through the power of the Holy Spirit and the instrumentality of the priest.

> *I am the living bread that came down from heaven; whoever eats this bread will live forever, and the bread that I will give is my flesh for the life of the world. For my flesh is true food, and my blood is true drink.* (John 6:51–55)

In the Catechism, we read:

> *The whole Christ is truly present, body, blood, soul, and divinity, under the appearances of bread and wine—the glorified Christ who rose from the dead after dying for our sins. This is what the Church means when she speaks of the "Real Presence" of Christ in the Eucharist.*
>
> *This presence of Christ in the Eucharist is called "real" not to exclude other types of his presence as if they could not be understood as real* (CCC no. 1374).

The risen Christ is present to His Church in many ways, but most profoundly through the sacrament of the Eucharist. For Catholics, "The Celebration of the Eucharist at Mass is defined as the "source and summit of the Christian life" (CCC 1324). In fact, the Eucharist is so cherished in the Catholic faith that it is the final sacrament given to a person who is about to die. The act of a priest giving the sacrament to a dying person is referred to as *viaticum*, a Latin term meaning: "provisions for the journey" or what is often called food for the journey. It is the final meal for the ultimate journey to the heavenly kingdom where the eternal banquet awaits all who believe.

According to the Catechism,

> The Christian who unites his own death to that of Jesus views it as a step towards him and an entrance into everlasting life. When the Church for the last time speaks Christ's words of pardon and absolution over the dying Christian, seals him for the last time with a strengthening anointing, and gives him Christ in viaticum as nourishment for the journey, she speaks with gentle assurance. (CCC 1020).

A beautiful prayer that is said for someone who is about to pass is the following:

> "Go forth, Christian soul, from this world
> in the name of God the almighty Father,
> who created you,
> in the name of Jesus Christ, the Son of
> the living God,
> who suffered for you, in the name of the

Holy Spirit,
who was poured out upon you.
Go forth, faithful Christian!

May you live in peace this day,
may your home be with God in Zion,
with Mary, the virgin Mother of God,
with Joseph, and all the angels and saints....

May you return to [your Creator]
who formed you from the dust of the earth.
May holy Mary, the angels, and all
the saints

come to meet you as you go forth from
this life....

May you see your Redeemer face to
face. Amen

In the future whenever you attend mass and receive Communion, remember the words of St. Agustine, who said, "Believe what you see, see what you believe and become what you are: the Body of Christ."

When we say "Amen," after receiving the Eucharist, we are saying "Yes! I believe this is the body, blood, soul, and divinity of Jesus Christ and that I will try to become the body of Christ to others. Become what you receive and recognize that when you and I receive the Eucharist, we are to look at the sacrament as the divine nourishment that will help us become the body of Christ.

As a devout Catholic himself, Tolkien wrote the following: "I put before you the one great thing to love on earth: the Blessed Sacrament (Eucharist)...There you will find romance, glory, honor, fidelity, and the true way of all your loves upon earth."

> Prayer: O my Jesus, I place myself in spirit before Thy Eucharistic Face to adore Thee, to make reparation, to say to Thee all that Thy Spirit of Love will cause to rise in my heart. I come to look at Thee. I come to listen to Thee. I come to receive from Thee all that Thy open Heart desires to say to me and to give me today. I thank Thee for having made Thyself close to me. I praise Thy mercy. I confess the redeeming power of Thy Precious Blood. Amen. O sweet Virgin Mary, I am thy child. Keep my hands in thy hands and my heart in thy heart all throughout this day and even during the night. So do I want to live and die. Amen.

Scripture for meditation

God commanded the skies above,
and opened the doors of heaven;
and he rained down upon them
manna to eat,
and gave them the bread of heaven.
Man ate the bread of the angels;
he sent them food in abundance. . . .
And they ate and were well filled,
for he gave them what they craved.

(Ps. 78:23–25, 29)

"Jesus said to them, "I am the bread of life; whoever comes to me shall not hunger, and whoever believes in me shall never thirst" (John 6:35).

"Truly, truly, I say to you, whoever believes has eternal life. I am the bread of life. Your fathers ate the manna in the wilderness, and they died. This is the bread that comes down from heaven, so that one may eat of it and not die" (John 6:47–50).

Chapter Nine:

Awareness Along the Journey

"For a lack of attention, a thousand forms of loveliness elude us every day" (**Evelyn Underhill**).

I was ordained a priest on June 2, 2001, in the parish I grew up in: Our Lady of Mercy on Long Island. It was a wonderful day with many family and friends in attendance along with my Oblate brothers, including Oblate Archbishop Roger Schweitz who ordained me. My first assignment took me to a wonderful multicultural parish in South Miami. The community was made up of families from over thirty countries, including Jamaica, Trinidad, Cuba, and Haiti. It was a joyful, fun-loving parish, and I will always treasure the four years I spent there!

On my days off, I would often head down to the key largo, about a 25-minute drive from the church to do some snorkeling. It was there where I encountered the famous 9-foot tall, 2,000-pound bronze statue titled *Christ of the Deep*.

Upon an Untrodden Path

The magnificent statue stands on the floor of the ocean at Key Largos John Pennekamp Coral Reef State Park. The statue was created by Guido Galletti in 1954 as a symbol to inspire all who explored and loved the sea. The sculpture depicts Jesus with outstretched arms, reaching toward the surface above. As one swims down toward the arms of Jesus, you get the feeling that He is just waiting for you to swim down and greet Him, allowing Him to pull you close to His sacred heart.

It has become a ritual of sorts for many to snorkel down and clutch the open hands of Jesus. For many years, there was a plaque attached to the base of the statue which is taken from Psalm 139:9:

> *"If I take the wings of the morning*
> *And dwell in the uttermost*
> *parts of the sea,*
> *Even there your hand will lead me*
> *and your right hand hold me fast."*

Awareness Along the Journey

For me, the sculpture is a reminder that we are never alone far from the gaze of our loving God, no matter where we find ourselves. A wonderful artist and dear friend from my former parish of St. Margaret Church in Monticello Florida named Susan Hopkins gifted me with a beautiful depiction of *Christ of the Deep*, which she painted. It hangs in my office across from my desk. I often refer to it when I am counseling people who feel that God isn't present to their needs and concerns.

In his book *Fruits of the Spirit*, Fr. Thomas Keating offers the following thought about recognizing the presence of God in our midst:

> The start, middle, and end of the spiritual journey is the conviction that God is always present. As we progress in this journey, we perceive God's presence more and more. The spiritual journey is a gradual process of enlarging our emotional, mental, and physical relationship with the Divine reality that is present in us but not ordinarily accessible to our emotions or concepts....We rarely think of the air we breathe, yet it is in us and around us all the time. In a similar fashion, the presence of God penetrates us, is all around us, is always embracing us. When I am at prayer in front of the Blessed Sacrament, I

> will recite a short prayer taken from scripture or another source from my faith. For example, I will repeat the following prayer throughout my time with Jesus, *God's life is living within me. I am aware of His life living within me.*

When people come to me for spiritual direction and are having a difficult time feeling Gods presence, I offer them some of the wisdom not only of Thomas Keating but of the great Carmelite mystic, St. Teresa of Avila who wrote: "All difficulties in prayer can be traced to one cause: praying as if God were absent." Very often, people come to adoration or settle in for a period of prayer and immediately begin to summon God to appear as if God were not already present in their midst. I have been guilty of that myself over the years, invoking God to make an appearance as if were rubbing a lamp, waiting for a genie to appear. I have at times forgotten the beautiful words of the psalmist: "Be still and know that am God" (Ps. 46:xx).

One of my favorite prayer cards is one inscribed with the well-known and comforting poem: "Footprints in the Sand." It was written in 1936 by a girl named Mary Stevenson who had lost her mother at age six. She grew up in poverty and hardship as her father struggled to raise eight children during the Great Depression. One cold winter's night when she was fourteen years old, Mary was locked out of the house. As she sat shivering on the doorstep, she wrote "Footprints" on a scrap of paper. As you read it, think about young Mary Stevenson struggling to find warmth, sitting out in the cold, and writing this. And think about what God, the good shepherd, was thinking as he watched over her that night.

One night I dreamed I was walking along the beach with the Lord. Many scenes from my life flashed across the sky. / In each scene I noticed footprints in the sand. /

Sometimes there were two sets of footprints, other times there was one set of footprints. / This bothered me because I noticed that during the low periods of my life, when I was suffering from anguish, sorrow or defeat, I could see only one set of footprints. /

So I said to the Lord, "You promised me, Lord, that if I followed you, you would walk with me always. / But I have noticed that during the most trying periods of my life there have only been one set of footprints in the sand. /

Why, when I needed you most, you have not been there for me." / The Lord replied, "The times when you have seen only one set of footprints in the sand, is when I carried you."

Ignatius of Loyola, founder of the Jesuits, implemented a practice of prayerful reflection on the events of the day in order to detect God's presence and discern his direction for us. The practice known as the "Examen," has helped many religious and laypeople become more aware of God's presence and see God's hand at work in our daily lives. St. Ignatius believed that the Examen was a gift that came directly from God and that God wanted it to be shared as widely as possible. The examen involves five steps toward growing in awareness of God's unconditional love and presence in our lives. The steps are as follows:

1. Become aware of God's presence.

2. Review the day with gratitude.

3. Pay attention to your emotions.

4. Look toward tomorrow.

5. Choose one feature of the day and pray from it.

The author of Hebrews reminds us,

> *Draw near to God with a sincere heart and with the full assurance that faith brings, having our hearts sprinkled to cleanse us from*

a guilty conscience and having our bodies washed with pure water. (Heb. 10:22)

Nicholas Herman (1611–1691) was born in the Lorraine region of France. After fighting in the Thirty Years War, he entered a Carmelite monastery in Paris in 1640 and took the religious name Lawrence of the Resurrection. Brother Lawrence, a seventeenth-century Carmelite friar, wrote a gem of a book entitled *The Practice of the Presence of God*. The book is a wonderful guide to bring to prayer. Regarding awareness of God's presence, Br. Lawrence writes the following:

> God does not ask much of us, merely a thought of Him from time to time, a little act of adoration, sometimes to ask for His grace, sometimes to offer Him your sufferings, at other times to thank Him for the graces, past and present, God has bestowed on you.
>
> In the midst of your troubles, take solace in Him as often as you can.
>
> Lift up your heart to Him during your meals; the least little remembrance will always be the most pleasing to Him. One

need not cry out very loudly; He is nearer to us than we think.

Brother Lawrence notes that "We need to give Jesus everything: our aversions, our suffering and the minutiae of our days." Brother Lawrence reminds us that "we must do this out of love, seeking no return, and to seek our satisfaction only in the fulfilling of His will, whether He leads us by suffering or by consolation. The more of ourselves we give to God, the more we will know His presence."

> *"Whether you eat or drink or whatever you do, do it all for the glory of God" (1 Cor. 10:31).*

Recognizing the presence of Our Lord along our journey of faith will bring us unimaginable comfort, consolation, and peace. As we begin each day, let us commit ourselves to tapping into the wealth of wisdom left to us by Ignatius of Loyola, Brother Lawrence, Teresa of Avila, Thomas Keating, and many others who have left us a rich legacy to follow. St. Augustine reminds us that we must also be present to God if we are to recognize his divine presence. He writes:

> You called, shouted, broke through my deafness; you flared, blazed, banished my blindness; you lavished your fragrance, I

gasped; and now I pant for you; I tasted you, and now I hunger and thirst; you touched me, and I burned for your peace.

Prayer: *O Lord, let me live with You as with a friend! Help me to live in the awareness of faith always, in order that I may be united to You no matter what happens. I bear heaven in my soul, since You, who satiate the blessed in the Beatific Vision, give Yourself to me in faith and mystery.*

Scripture for meditation

"For in Him we live and move and exist, as even some of your own poets have said, 'For we also are His children" (Acts 17:28).

"The next day he saw Jesus coming to him and said, "Behold, the Lamb of God who takes away the sins of the world" (John 1:29).

"Simon Peter answered him, 'Lord, to whom shall we go? You have the words of eternal life, and we have believed, and have come to know, that you are the Holy One of God.'"(John 6:68–69)

Chapter Ten

Perseverance

"It does not matter how slowly you go so long as you do not stop" (Confucius, 551–479 BC).

There is a story of a woman who visited a monastery and asked the abbot what the monks do in there all day. The abbot responded, "We fall down, get up, and fall down again." It is a simple illustration that captures the journey for many of us, which is a lifelong journey of falling down and getting up again.

One of the classic definitions of perseverance is a belief that through prayer, and good works we will develop an understanding that God not only wants to be involved in our lives but that he will help us carry our cross when feel we can no longer persevere. Remember the words of Jesus himself:

> *Come to me, all you who are weary and burdened, and I will give you rest. Take my yoke upon you and learn from me, for I am gentle and humble in heart, and you will find rest for your souls. For my yoke is easy and my burden is light. (Matt. 11:28–30)*

I have always been a big fan of adventure stories; both fiction and nonfiction. Hemingway and London are among my favorite authors. But when it comes to the theme of perseverance along the journey, the story that immediately comes to mind, is that of *The Endurance*. Sir Ernest Shackleton (1874–1922) was a famous Irish-born British explorer who set his sights on being the first man to reach the South Pole in Antarctica. Shackelton first attempted the journey with the famous British explorer Robert Falcon Scott in 1901, but illness forced the team to abandon the attempt and return to England. In 1907, Shackelton made a second, but it too failed, due to fierce winds and extreme drops in temperature. Finally In 1914 Sir Ernest Shackleton lead a twenty-eight men crew on a third Trans-Antarctic Expedition. The expedition intended to transverse the Antarctic continent by dog sled.

In December of that year the expedition, aboard the purpose-built polar exploration ship, *Endurance*, entered the packed ice of the Weddell Sea off the coast of Antarctica some 1,100 nautical miles east of the Palmer Peninsula. By January,1915, Endurance was a scant sixty nautical miles from its intended landfall—but it was also frozen, immobile, trapped in packed ice that extended to all horizons. Endurance drifted with the pack ice for several months, eventually losing sight of land as the Weddell Sea current spun the vast packed-ice floe in a slow clockwise direction. By late October,1915, Endurance would drift some 500 nautical miles to the northeast, frozen fast in apparently limitless pack ice. In the intervening months, the crew would lead a life of many trials and tribulations amidst the intense cold. As the weather turned ever colder, the packed ice thickened, and winter storms drove the floes together with increasing pressure and violence. At the end of October, 1915, the *Endurance* would finally succumb to the intense pressure and would be slowly crushed.

The crew, led by Shackleton, abandoned the *Endurance* and made camp on a huge floe of packed ice. They would salvage as much food and materials as possible, along with the expedition's dogs, sleds, and boats, which would be stockpiled on the floe. The crew would establish a makeshift home and named the drifting flow, "Ocean Camp."

The *Endurance* would finally slip entirely beneath the sea; meanwhile the initial floe would crumble under pressure, and the crew would have to relocate to a larger, sturdier ice flow. Shackelton would eventually decide to depart in three small boats for Elephant Island off the southern tip of Cape Horn. They would arrive at Elephant Island seven days later, but the island would be uninhabited and far from shipping lanes. Shackleton would eventually set out in a lifeboat with a team of five men and, several weeks later, he would arrive at South Georgia and organize a rescue of the rest of his crew on August 25, 1916. They'd been stranded for two years and, miraculously, not one of the twenty-eight-member crew died.

Shackleton eventually mounted a fourth attempt to reach the South Pole in late 1921 and died of a heart attack on his ship in 1922. He never made it. Before his death, Sir Ernest would write the following in his journal:

> When I look back at those days I have no doubt that Providence guided us, not only across those snowfields, but across the storm-white sea that separated Elephant Island from our landing-place on South Georgia. I know that during that long and racking march of thirty-six hours over the unnamed mountains and glaciers of South Georgia it seemed to me often that we were four, not three of us.

Perseverance

It could be argued that a lot of what drove Shackleton was pride and the seeking of fame and recognition of his peers. Many, including myself would like to think of Sir Ernest Shackleton as a man who epitomized perseverance along a journey!" It is said that Sir Ernest placed an ad in the paper, looking for men willing to embark on the remarkable and ill-fated journey on the *Endurance*. The ad read as follows: "Men wanted for hazardous journey. Low wages, bitter cold, long hours of complete darkness. Safe return doubtful. Honor and recognition in event of success." Talk about answering a call to persevere on a journey!

Over the years of being a pastor, spiritual director, confessor, and counselor, people tell me that at times, that it feels as if God is not helping them persevere during their own trials and challenges. Sometimes, in the face of suffering in all its forms, it seems hard for many to feel God's healing touch, comfort, consolation, and unconditional love. Part of our human nature is that we can easily abandon a pursuit of any kind if we find that it is not bearing fruit right away, and that includes our spiritual life. People will confess to me in spiritual direction, that they don't "feel any growth occurring while they pray the rosary or the divine mercy chaplet or sit in adoration before the Blessed Sacrament. I encourage them to stay with it, assuring them that growth and transformation are occurring within. They may not see any physical signs of growth, but the growth is occurring beneath the surface in the heart, mind, and soul during their time of prayer.

One illustration that I have used while giving homilies and in direction, is one of the "Moso bamboo tree" that grows in the forests of China and Taiwan. It is a fascinating tree. The year of planting its seed, there are no visible signs of growth. In the second year, again, no growth above the soil. The third and the fourth year, still no growth. It is an exercise in perseverance and patience for those who tend these amazing trees.

Like those of us who pray continuously, we wonder if our efforts will ever be rewarded. Finally, in the fifth year, one will witness an explosion of growth! The Moso Bamboo Tree will grow eighty feet in just six weeks! An amazing feat to be sure! The key to this amazing tree is that while it looks like the tree is remaining dormant during those four years, the tree has been developing a deep and strong root system that will support the massive tree as it grows!

A similar principle can be applied to our spiritual growth. As we sit patiently in prayer and adoration, God's Word is taking root in our receptive hearts, which will help us grow in our love, faith, and trust in Jesus Christ. This is how you and I become the children God created us to be.

An extraordinary book I read this past year is entitled, *In Sinu Jesu*. It is a book of private revelations, in which our Lord and our Blessed Mother speak to a Benedictine monk who keeps a journal of these extraordinary revelations. In one encounter, Jesus speaks to the monk with these loving words:

> It is My Heart that waits for you in the tabernacle; it is My gaze that, full of tenderness, fixes itself, from the tabernacle, on those who draw near to it. I am not there for My own sake. I am there to feed you and to fill you with the joys of My presence. I am He who understands every man's loneliness, especially the loneliness of My priests. I want to share their loneliness, so that they will not be alone with themselves, but alone with Me.
>
> There I shall speak to their hearts as I am speaking to you. I am ablaze to be for each one of My priests the Friend whom they seek, the Friend with whom they can share everything.

Beautiful words and a beautiful promise to all who come away to rest in the Lord.

In the smash-hit Broadway musical "Godspell" one of the hit songs from the musical is "Day by Day." The lyrics include the these words

Day by day
Oh Dear Lord
Three things I pray
To see thee more clearly
Love thee more dearly
Follow thee more nearly
Day by day

The song became a big hit on the charts, but what many people may not be aware of is the song was taken from a prayer composed by a thirteenth-century priest, Richard, Bishop of Chichester in AD 1253. I have recommended this prayer to people having difficulty persevering in prayer and recognizing Jesus dwelling in their midst. Although the prayer is a brief one, it contains everything necessary to grow closer to God and become more aware of his loving presence.

One of the Gospel scenes that resonates with a lot of people struggling to persevere is the scene where the apostles are being tossed about in a storm, and Jesus seems completely oblivious to the crisis as he sleeps peacefully on a cushion in the boat. *"Waves crash into the boat so that the boat is being swamped. But he (Jesus) was...asleep on the cushion, and they woke him up and said to him, '...do you not care that we are perishing?"* (Mark 4:37–39). Very often people feel that Jesus is asleep on the proverbial cushion when they come to Him in their time when very little perseverance is left in their tank. Nothing can be further from the truth!

The great mystic and saint Padre Pio offers these comforting words during such times: "Stay in the boat in which our Lord has placed you, and let the storm come. You will not perish. It appears to you that Jesus is sleeping, but let it be so. Don't you know that if He sleeps, His heart vigilantly watches over you. Let Him sleep, but at the right time, He will awaken to restore your calm."

A story is told about the noted director of biblical epics, Cecil B. DeMille. When he and the film crew began working on the movie *Ben Hur*, DeMille talked to Charlton Heston—the star of the movie—about the all-important chariot race that would become one of the great scenes in cinematic history. DeMille decided that Heston should actually learn to drive the chariot himself, rather than relying on a stunt double. Heston agreed to take chariot-driving lessons to make the scene as authentic as possible. Learning to drive a chariot with horses four abreast, however, was no small task. After extensive work and days of practice, Heston returned to the movie set and reported to DeMille. "I think I can drive the chariot all right, Cecil," said Heston, "but I'm not at all sure I can actually win the race."

Smiling slightly, DeMille said, "Charlton, you just stay on the chariot, and I'll make sure you win the race."

I love that story for many reasons, not only is it funny, but more importantly it is a wonderful illustration of the call to persevere in order to win the unfading crown of glory.

As Saint Paul reminds us, *"We are all called to run the good race in such a way as to get the prize"* (1 Cor. 9:24). I can imagine Jesus beside us telling us each day to "stay on that chariot, using your gifts and talents to meet the needs and concerns of our brothers and sisters, and I will make sure you win the race!"

> Prayer: Grant me, O Lord, my God, a mind to know You, a heart to seek You, wisdom to find You, conduct pleasing to You, faithful perseverance in waiting for You, and a hope of finally embracing You. Amen (St. Thomas Aquinas).

Scripture for meditation

> *"As you know, we count as blessed those who have persevered. You have heard of Job's perseverance and have seen what the Lord finally brought about. The Lord is full of compassion and mercy." (James 5:11)*

> *"Therefore, since we are surrounded by such a great cloud of witnesses, let us throw off everything that hinders and the sin that so easily entangles. And let us run with perseverance the race marked out for us. (Heb. 12:1)*

Chapter Eleven

The Interior Journey

"The unexamined life is not worth living" (Plato)

I once attended a talk given by Fr. Thomas Keating. In one of his talks, he who pointed out that *"Silence is God's language, and it's a very difficult language to learn."* It is hard to grasp the concept that silence can be looked upon as a language, yet communion with God in moments of silence, has the potential to be a far more transformative experience than words can often bring us. I often encourage people during spiritual direction, not to be afraid of silent communication with God. Do not feel as though you must speak or even hear what He has to say. Simply being silent, in His presence, knowing that He is there, may be exactly what your soul is in need of in those moments.

Great mystics, saints and spiritual writers over the centuries have been writing and speaking about the interior life of silent prayer and meditation, a life of seeking a deeper and more profound relationship with God while growing in virtue and holiness. Thomas Merton wrote extensively about the inner journey. He writes, "As for me, I have but one desire, the desire for solitude. To be lost in the secret of God's face." (The Sign of Jonah)

In the remarkable diary, *The Divine Mercy*, St. Maria Faustina Kowalska kept a remarkable and inspiring diary based on the private revelations she received from Jesus. This deeply prayerful soul, wrote this prayer:

> Lord, I desire to seek You and know You. Help me to hear You speak through the silence. Help me to understand this deep language of love and to allow You to transform me through this form of prayer. I love You, dear Lord, and I desire to rest in Your Heart. Jesus, I trust in You.

It is so important to take that time each day for quiet reflection and meditation. Many mystics, saints, and other prayerful souls refer to this practice of coming away to a quiet place as the "prayer of inner silence." The prayer of inner silence is a way for one to develop a lovingly receptive heart, a heart that is able to hear that inner voice of God says to us, "Be still and know that I am God" (Ps. 46:10).

Sr. Wendy Beckett, a well-known Carmelite nun who wrote many books on religious art and prayer writes the following:

> In silent prayer, there are no words and hence no thoughts. We are still. This silence is nothing to be afraid of. Five or ten minutes, whatever can be spared. You are just there to stand or kneel in His presence and let Him take possession of you.

I have found that quiet time with Jesus at the end of a busy day to be a wonderful way to decompress and rest in the Lord. Learning the language of silence is indeed challenging, particularly in a world in we are surrounded by a cacophony of noises. Many pastors like myself are immensely blessed to have a private chapel with the Blessed Sacrament in our residences, a place to come away to the quiet.

In his wonderful and inspiring book, *The Wedding Feast at Cana in Galilee*, Fr. Thomas Keating offers his wisdom to those who seek to embark on an inward journey and learn the language of God. He writes the following: "How can I be a contemplative in everyday life, with its noise, turmoil, and constant interruptions. How can I be interiorly quiet when the world is getting noisier and the pace of life faster." The answer is to slow down and pray more. Prayer has the great advantage of giving us a perspective on what we have to do. If we practice contemplative prayer every day, we find that we have more time for everything else." Contemplative prayer cultivates the gift of discernment. Spiritual discernment is not something we have to try to do; it arises spontaneously as one of the fruits of the Spirit communicated to us during contemplative prayer.

The most significant source of security, independence, and true love is the firm conviction that the divine Trinity—Father, Son, and Holy Spirit—dwells within us all the time, twenty-four hours a day, under all circumstances, and is available to us at any time." One of the most moving and profound scripture passages of the call to the interior can be found in the book of the prophet Hosea who brings this beautiful message of our God to his people. *"I will lead her into the desert where I will speak to her heart"*(Hos. 2:14). The image of the desert is often used to describe the inner journey; the journey of going inward is the journey toward silence away from the frenetic pace and noise of the secular culture. In his work, *Pensées* Blaise Pascal observed, "All the problems of men arises from one single fact, that they cannot stay quietly in their chamber." St. Teresa of Calcutta recognized the value of silence and the inner life with Jesus. The diminutive nun would often pass out little prayer cards to visitors with the words: *"Prayer is the fruit of silence; faith is the fruit of prayer; love is the fruit of faith; service is the fruit of love."* It is a beautiful summation as it follows a sequence. Silence leads to prayer, which leads to faith, then to love, and finally to serving others. It is calling to gradually move each day from worship to serving others.

Years ago, on a rare rainy day in San Antonio (very rare, by the way!), I decided to check out a movie playing at one of the small art house theaters near my parish. I had heard about this very unusual and interesting film entitled *Into Great Silence*. The film is a two and a half-hour look inside the walls of La Grande Chartreuse—the great charterhouse in the Alps outside Grenoble—where St. Bruno founded the Carthusians in 1084. The film gives the viewer a rare look into the daily rhythm of life that defines a Carthusian monk. There is no narration or commentary during the film. The screen is filled with the sound of silence.

Philip Gröning, the German director who took on this unique project, was amazed by such a life of detachment and commitment to God exhibited by the monks. During the shooting of the film, Gröning was given permission by the Abbot to live among the monks. While shooting the film, Gröning lived and prayed and worked with the monks. Gröning remarked

> Carthusian monks are vowed to the strictest silence, They live in small cells with straw beds, and as a stove, all they have is a little tin box; you freeze immediately if you let the fire go out. Each day is so highly structured, as monks meet up to chant the Divine Office and for the Holy

Sacrifice of the Mass. Their life is one of
the most severe simplicity and asceticism.

Gröning also commented:

> The Carthusians live in great poverty, but
> they are consciously poor. For example,
> the tailor keeps every button and every
> scrap of fabric. When a monk dies, his
> buttons are re-used. In the film, there is a
> scene where we see the button collection
> in the tailor's shop. There are also boxes
> of threads, and even the smallest usable
> bits and pieces of a monk's habit are recycled.
> If you look at the habits closely, you
> can see that they are often pieced together
> from countless patches. Basically, nothing
> is ever thrown away. And all the income
> that has not been spent by the end of the
> year is donated. They thus never have a
> surplus of money.

As I watched the film, I noticed that there was not a sound made by any of the other moviegoers, including me. It seemed like the silence of monks on the screen had an infectious effect on all of us. I think we were all fascinated by the spirit of detachment and the commitment of theses monks, who are living in our world but not being of our world as our Lord Jesus taught. These men have chosen the interior journey as they seek a deeper communion with their Lord. It truly is a beautiful vocation and journey.

Cardinal Robert Sarah commented that "Monasteries are places where one learns to live and die in an atmosphere of silent prayer, the gaze always turned toward the beyond toward the One who made us and whom we contemplate." Let us set aside time each day and rest in the presence of the Lord.

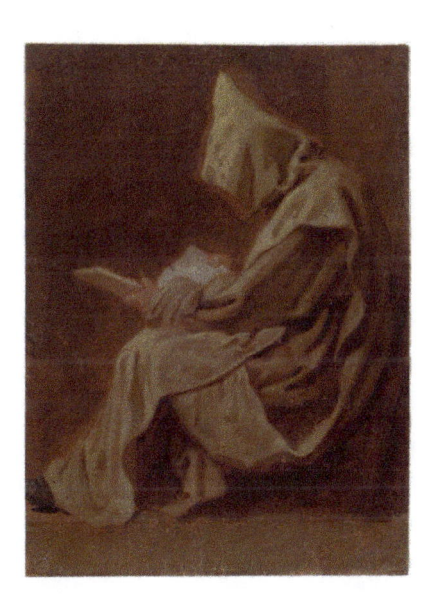

Prayer: Father, Son, and Holy Spirit, help me to know You and to love You. Help me to discover the love You share within Your own divine life. In that discovery, help me also to love others with Your heart. Father, Son, and Holy Spirit, I trust in You.

Scripture for meditation

"Rejoice constantly, pray ceaselessly, give thanks in all circumstances...Do not quench the Spirit" (1 Thess 5:16ff.).

"For in Him, we live and move and have our being" (Acts 17:28).

"yet I live, no longer I, but Christ lives in me; insofar as I now live in the flesh, I live by faith in the Son of God who has loved me and given himself up for me" (Gal. 2:12).

Chapter Twelve

Time

"God created time, and He created plenty of it" (Old Irish proverb).

The author of that proverb, must have been a hermit living in a desert cave, away from the frenetic pace of the culture most of us find ourselves immersed in. I do agree that God did give us his children plenty of time to find our purpose in life. Unfortunately, many people seem to be wasting a lot of that precious time on meaningless and forgettable distractions and empty pursuits. In our moment in history, many people are spending countless hours on social media, texting on their cell phone, and so on. In addition to our gadgets, binge-watching Netflix, Prime, and pay-per-view movies and series are also becoming a very significant part of a person's twenty-four-hour day.

At times, I have found myself up past midnight telling myself "Just one more episode, and then I'll go to bed...I just have to find out what happens." It finally dawned on me that I was allowing so much of my precious time to be eaten up with the empty calories of TV.

Procrastination is another time consumer that affects many of us as well. English writer Edward Young penned the proverb "Procrastination is the thief of time." Procrastination, along with laziness and poor choices, can gobble up our time like a Pac Man arcade game. On the other end of the spectrum, are the multitaskers. Those who pursue so many projects, goals, and objectives simultaneously that they often find themselves with little or no time to address their physical, emotional, and spiritual needs and concerns. A sense of urgency seems to be the constant companion for many of us as we journey through life. Speaking for myself, I often worry, that I am not using my time wisely as the sands of time quickly fill my proverbial hourglass.

Well-known author Abraham Joshua Herschel writes, "The higher goal of spiritual living is not to amass a wealth of information, but to face sacred moments. Spiritual life begins to decay when we fail to sense the grandeur of what is eternal in time." God's Word advises us to use our time wisely because He knows that many things in life can distract us from what truly matters. Do not waste your days trying to prolong them, so that you do not look back with a sense of sadness and lost opportunity.

One of my favorite authors, Jack London, wrote a beautiful poem that I keep on the wall of my office. It reminds me of the importance of not wasting the gift of time God has given me! The poem reads as follows:

I would rather be ashes than dust!

I would rather that my spark should burn out in a brilliant blaze than it should be stifled by dry-rot.

I would rather be a superb meteor, every atom of me in magnificent glow, than a sleepy and permanent planet.

The function of man is to live, not to exist.

I shall not waste my days trying to prolong them.

I shall use my time.

Jack London certainly did use his time well with several best-selling novels, short stories, and poems attributed to him, including *Call of the Wild*, *White Fang*, *Martin Eden*, and *The Sea Wolf* just to name a few.

Sadly, I fear many sparks of potential greatness are being stifled by dry rot, as time marches on and many people continue to distracted by vices and empty pursuits that keep them in a state of arrested development. One of my favorite sayings was written by St. Irenaeus, who wrote, *"The glory of God is the man (woman) fully alive!"* We should strive to be fully alive and striving to become the men and women

God created them to be. Some of the well-known parables of Jesus remind us not to waste our time on selfish pursuits and to engage in vices and behaviors that militate against the values of the Gospels. The parable of the talents comes to mind for me as I think about the passage of time in one's life and how best to use one's time.

> *For it will be like a man going on a journey, who called his servants[a] and entrusted to them his property. To one, he gave five talents,[b] to another two, to another one, to each according to his ability. Then he went away. He who had received the five talents went at once and traded with them, and he made five talents more. So also he who had the two talents made two talents more. But he who had received the one talent went and dug in the ground and hid his master's money.*
>
> *Now after a long time, the master of those servants came and settled accounts with them. And he who had received the five talents came forward, bringing five talents more, saying, "Master, you delivered to me five talents; here, I have made five talents more." His master said to him, "Well done, good and faithful servant.[c] You have been faithful over a little; I*

will set you over much. Enter into the joy of your master."

And he also who had the two talents came forward, saying, "Master, you delivered to me two talents; here, I have made two talents more." His master said to him, "Well done, good and faithful servant. You have been faithful over a little; I will set you over much. Enter into the joy of your master."

He also who had received the one talent came forward, saying, "Master, I knew you to be a hard man, reaping where you did not sow, and gathering where you scattered no seed, so I was afraid, and I went and hid your talent in the ground. Here, you have what is yours." But his master answered him, "You wicked and slothful servant! You knew that I reap where I have not sown and gather where I scattered no seed. Then you ought to have invested my money with the bankers, and at my coming, I should have received what was my own with interest. So take the talent from him and give it to him who has the ten talents." For everyone who has will more be given, and he will have an abundance. But from the one who has not, even what he has will be taken away. (Matt. 25:14–29)

The parable is not only a sobering reminder of how fleeting time is, it also captures the beautiful truth that we are created out of love, equipped with many gifts and talents to be used, not only for God's greater glory, but also to help meet the needs and concerns of others in need. For myself, the parable of the talents is an excellent passage for mediation and discernment. It has helped me to confront my mortality and realize that all is a gift, and I should be using my gifts and talents to honor God and reach out to those in need.

The academy award-winning film, *Chariots of Fire* (1981), is the true story of two gifted athletes who compete for the gold in the 1924 Olympic Games in Paris, France. One runner, England's Harold Abrahams, the son of Lithuanian Jewish parents, is gifted with great speed. Harold, who has not lived a privileged life, has achieved the goal of becoming a student at Cambridge University, thanks to the sacrifices of his family and his own determination. Harold uses his athletic prowess to overcome what he sees as a culture of anti-Semitic leanings at the university. In one scene, Harold comments, "Here I am often invited to the trough but not allowed to drink. Harold's amazing speed in the 100- and 200-meter events eventually earns him the respect of his classmates, and faculty members.

The other main character in the story is Eric Liddell, a Scotsman who is a devout missionary of the Church of Scotland. Eric sees running as a way of spreading the good news of the Gospel. As the fastest runner in Scotland, Eric draws vast crowds of fans to his events. Eric gathers his fans before his races to evangelize whenever possible. Eric sees his speed as being a gift from God, and he wants to run to honor God with his talent! In one very moving scene in the movie, Eric explains to his sister Jenny, "God made me fast. And when I run, I feel His pleasure!" Both Harold and Eric will eventually become rivals under the same flag, representing Great Britain, and both men will bring home the gold (Harold in the 100 meters and Eric in the 400 meters).

After seeing this amazing film, I found it very inspiring to see these two men so dedicated, who sacrificed so much to achieve something incredible! Eric Liddell, in particular was indeed a man fully alive who gave all the glory to God. Eric would eventually lay down his life, being killed in a mission in China.

Prayer: Dear Lord, when I complete my earthly pilgrimage and kneel before your throne of justice, may I hear those beautiful words, "Well done, my good and faithful servant."

Scripture for meditation

"He has made everything beautiful in its time. He has also set eternity in the human heart, yet no one can fathom what God has done from beginning to end" (Eccles. 3:11).

"Yet you do not know what tomorrow will bring. What is your life? For you are a mist that appears for a little time and then vanishes" (James 4:14).

But about that day or hour no one knows, not even the angels in heaven, nor the Son, but only the Father. Be on guard! Be alert! You do not know when that time will come" (Mark 13:32–33).

Chapter Thirteen

Signs

"There's a great deal to say in the Bible about the signs we're to watch for, and when these signs all converge in one place, we can be sure that we're close to the end of the age" (Rev Billy Graham).

Many people are familiar with the story of the man who is trapped on the roof of his house while a flood rages around him. He prays to God for deliverance. A short time later, a small boat motors down the flooded street. The man prefers to stay where he is, confident that God will save him.

Soon after, with the floodwaters continuing to engulf the house, a larger boat offers to evacuate him. Declining once again, the man is sure that he should stay where he is, so convinced that God will come to his rescue.

The rains continue, and the water rises. As the torrent engulfs the house, the man climbs to the top of the chimney. While there, awaiting God's intervention, a rescue helicopter lowers a ladder, but the man declines the help. "I know that God will save me," he says to the pilot.

Inevitably, the man has been swept away in the water and drowns. When he appears before God, the man is sorely disappointed. "I had such confidence in you, Lord," he says, "How could you abandon me."

"Abandon you." God replies. "What more could you want. I sent you two boats and a helicopter!"

Signs are very much a part of our identity as Christians. Jesus himself spoke of the importance of paying attention to the signs of the times (see Luke 12:56). Do you ever wish that God would send you a sign from heaven as a way of giving you reassurance, confidence, guidance, and direction in life? Do we look for signs from God and rely upon them? Do we shrug off signs as mere coincidences or fail to take time to that these signs may be from above?

Lake Tahoe—Big Blue, as it is referred to by many—is North America's largest alpine lake and the jewel of the High Sierras. Each year, the Nevada Commission on Tourism holds the annual seventy-two-mile Tour de Tahoe cycling event. I was able to enter and ride the course on two occasions, which circumnavigates the highways around Lake Tahoe in both Nevada and California. It includes a challenging 800-foot climb to a rest stop overlooking Emerald Bay and a 1,000-foot climb to Spooner Junction. There are also many beautiful views with rolling hills, ascents, and descents. It is both an exhilarating and challenging ride.

One year, I was joined by two close friends, Liz and John, who are parishioners at St. Mary's. Liz, a retired detective with the city of San Antonio and John, a retired fireman, were welcome companions as we embarked on the Tour de Tahoe. Although all three of us have kept in good shape over the years, Liz was only beginning to add cycling to her fitness routine. The three of us stayed together throughout the ride, enjoying the scenic views and good conversation. John and I were very proud and impressed with Liz who had chosen this challenging ride as her baptism by fire into the cycling world. By mile 65, many riders, including the three of us were dealing with issues, including stitches, lactic acid build-up, fatigue, and dehydration. Throughout the race, Liz had been praying to St. Michael the Archangel to keep us safe and get us to the finish line. As we approached the home stretch on mile 70, we noticed a street sign that read "St. Michael's Ct." The three of us looked at each and agreed it was a confirmation that St. Michael had heard Liz's prayer. As faithful Catholics, we had no doubt that this street sign was indeed a heavenly one as well! After a good laugh we raised our hands to heaven, thanking God for a blessed day of riding, while enjoying spectacular views of His creation!

Signs of God's presence are not only found in humorous or ordinary situations. They are very often found in times of great tragedy and suffering. On the morning of Sept. 11, 2001, Al Qaeda terrorists hijacked four commercial airliners. Two planes were deliberately flown into the twin towers in lower Manhattan. A second flight was flown into the Pentagon in Washington, DC, and several brave passengers thwarted a third attempted hijacking on United flight 93 as they overpowered the hijackers, giving their lives and preventing another potential act of terror. It was a day no one will ever forget. In the aftermath of the horror, the lives of nearly 3,000 people were taken. Millions around the world turned to God, looking for comfort, consolation, healing, and peace.

My family was impacted in a very personal way as I lost a beloved member of my family, Walter (Wally) Travers who had married my first cousin Rosemary. Cantor Fitzgerald lost 658 employees in the September 11 attacks—nearly a fourth of all the victims. Its offices were in the North Tower on the 101st through 105th floors. Wally, who was a broker at the firm and was working in the North Tower of the trade center when the first plane, American Airlines flight 11 struck. Wally, along with many others, were trapped above the impact zone, which cut off any possibility of rescue or escape. As I grieved over the loss of Wally, I was so thankful that my brother in-law, Kevin, who is married to my sister, Diane, was working in the South Tower and was able to exit the building before the second highjacked plane, United Airlines flight 175 was flown into the south tower. Both towers eventually collapsed, killing many more people, including our brave firefighters, police officers, and other first responders.

Signs

At the time, I had been ordained a priest only three short months, and was beginning my first assignment at Christ the King parish in Miami. Both Wally and Rosemary, were present at my ordination. The thought never entered my mind that I would never see him again after that beautiful day of celebration and joy. Another unimaginable thought was that the first funeral I would be presiding at as a newly ordained priest, would be for Wally who was laid to rest near his home parish in New Jersey.

In the midst of the worst terrorist attack on the US mainland in our nation's history, millions watched helplessly as our fellow citizens died in the World Trade Center, the Pentagon, and Shanksville, Pennsylvania. As a dark cloud hung over the country following the terrorist attacks, the light of a God's presence began to emerge among the smoldering wreckage of lower Manhattan. The most memorable and moving of these signs was the now-famous "Cross at Ground Zero." For those not familiar with the story, one of the excavation crew members named Frank Silechhia discovered the now famous "Cross" on September 13, 2001, two days after the terrorist attacks, as he was searching through the smoldering wreckage of twisted steel and concrete for human remains. A seventeen-foot-long crossbeam, weighing over two tons, was thrust at a vertical angle in the midst of the rubble. The cross was pulled from the wreckage and erected on a concrete abutment. It would become a great symbol of hope, healing, and comfort for the millions of people who were grieving the loss of their loved ones, friends, and co-workers. The cross was soon blessed, and religious services from many different Christian denominations, including the Catholic Mass, began to be held at the base of the Cross. Each night, illuminated by backlighting, the cross shone over the smoking debris as rescue workers kept searching for victims. The cross is now on display at the 9/11 Memorial & Museum in lower Manhattan. The museum is an educational and historical institution, honoring the victims and preserving the memories of 9/11 through artifacts, pictures, and recordings of the day's' events.

As I walked through the museum with my brother, Joe, we were both moved by the images, especially the personal items found and placed in glass cases, including women's shoes, watches, purses, briefcases, and even a doll that most likely belonged to a child on one of the hijacked flights. In a nearby room was a crushed fire truck, an engine from one of the highjacked planes, and the Cross of Ground Zero. After Joe and I left the memorial, we headed to the reflecting pool to search for the names of people we knew personally, including Wally, and other people we knew through our siblings, relatives, and friends. The names of those who died are etched in the marble along the perimeter of the pool. When we found Wally's name, we paused to pray for his and all the souls of those who lost their lives on that tragic day. As Joe and I were leaving, a glimmering stone that was left on the memorial caught my eye. The stone looked like a polished river stone. A piece of paper was tucked beneath it. I carefully picked up the stone along with the paper underneath.

The paper contained a handwritten verse from scripture which read:

> *"Can a mother forget the baby at her breast and have no compassion on the child she has borne. Though she may forget, I will not forget you! See, I have engraved you on the palm of my hand"(Isa. 49:15).*

Ask God to increase within you the gift of discernment, faith, and trust, rather than seeking God in signs. Jesus awaits us in the Blessed Sacrament, in creation, at prayer, in the sacraments, and at the Holy Mass..

I often offer these passages in spiritual direction to assure people that signs of God's presence are wonderful when experienced. However, even if we fail to see those divine signs, we should always be assured that it is in prayer that God hears our pleas and concerns (Ps. 34:15; 2 Chron. 7:14). It is also in His promise that God will never abandon us (Deut. 31:8), and it is in His wisdom that God knows what is most beneficial for us (Matt. 6:8; Luke 11:13).

> Prayer: Oh Light of the World, infinite God, Father of Eternity, the giver of wisdom and knowledge and ineffable dispenser of every spiritual grace; who knowest all things before they are made, who makes the darkness and the light; put forth Thy hand and touch my mouth and make it as a sharp sword to utter Thy Words eloquently.

Scripture for meditation

> *"This beginning of His signs, Jesus did in Cana of Galilee and manifested His glory, and His disciples believed in Him" (John 2:11).*

"As He was sitting on the Mount of Olives, the disciples came to Him privately, saying, 'Tell us, when will these things happen, and what will be the sign of Your coming, and the end of the age'" (Matt. 24:3).

"Ask a sign for yourself from the Lord your God; make it deep as Sheol or high as heaven" (Isa. 7:11).

Chapter Fourteen

Companions on the Journey

"No one is useless in this world who lightens
the burdens of another" (Charles Dickens).

Why did Jesus send out the disciples in pairs rather than individually? (Mark 6:7). We know that Jesus himself promised "For where two or three gather in my name, there am I with them"(Matt. 18:20). In addition to the welcome company, companions can offer encouragement, support, and even levity at times. They can support one another, and even be a source of comfort at times. This intention of having companions along our journey has been part of God's plan from the beginning of creation as we read in the book of Genesis: *"The Lord God said, 'It is not good for the man to be alone. I will make a helper suitable for him'"(Gen. 2:18).* God, in His infinite wisdom, recognized the importance of spouses, families, friendships, and companions to lean on, laugh with, and love!

The Bible is a rich deposit of stories, illustrating journeys and those who traveled those journeys together. Think of Moses and Aaron (Exod. 4:14–16), Elijah and Elisha (1 Sam. 18:1–5), Peter and Andrew (Matt. 4:18),

James and John (Matt. 4:21), and Mary and Joseph (Luke 1:39–56). For many people, the disciples on the Road to Emmaus encountering Jesus is among the most endearing stories of companions on a journey.

Many of us have had the opportunity to travel both alone and with companions, and for many, traveling with companions is the preferred option of travel. Walking with others along my own journey of faith has been both rewarding and enriching experience. Making lasting memories while sharing life experiences with someone has always been a source of great joy for me. I think about all the family vacations, pilgrimages, road trips, and so on that have been among the most memorable and joyful experiences of my life.

Having family, friends, and fellow sojourners to share our journeys with often leads to lifelong bonds and a deepening of love and friendship with our brothers and sisters in Christ. In addition to our earthly companions who accompany us on our way, God, in his infinite love and care, has given us the gift of the Saints to call upon to be a great source of companionship.

I have found it quite amazing and heartening to meet so many people who have chosen a particular Saint to be their go-to companion as they navigate their way through the joys and sorrows, the trials and tribulations, and moments of darkness and light that are a part of life. Pope Emeritus Benedict XVI, once described Saint Joseph as his "traveling companion" in life and ministry.

My parents, Robert and Teresa, met for the very first time while attending a daily mass that concluded with the Miraculous Medal Novena. This devotion to our Blessed Mother and the miraculous medal has remained an essential part of their lives ever since. My father always wore the miraculous medal up until the day he passed away. The medal is now worn by my younger brother Joe.

In the private revelations given by Jesus in the book, *In Sinu Jesu*, Jesus lovingly tells a humble monk the following:

> I never wanted to leave you alone on earth; this is why I have always surrounded you with My saints. I wanted, and want still, that you should find in them a true friendship, a friendship that is all pure, a friendship that does not disappoint.
>
> Through the saints and by their ceaseless intercession for you before My Face, you will, at length, come to Me in glory. Do not cease invoking My saints and teach others to seek from them the help they need in the trials of this life on earth. In heaven, the saints will all be glad for having helped you make your way to Me in glory.

In addition to our holy saints, God has assigned to each one of us a guardian angel to accompany us on every step of our earthly journey from our birth to our final breath. It is hard to grasp the idea that God has blessed each of us with these ethereal creatures who have been by our side or (on our shoulder) since our birth. In the Catechism we read:

> From its beginning until death, human life is surrounded by their watchful care and intercession. Beside each believer stands an angel as protector and shepherd leading him to life. Already here on earth, the Christian life shares by faith in the blessed company of angels and men united in God. [CCC 336]

In his Angelus address on Oct 2, 2011, then Pope Emeritus Benedict XVI stated the following:

> Dear friends, the Lord is ever close and active in humanity's history, and accompanies us with the unique presence of his Angels, whom today the Church venerates as "Guardian Angels," that is, ministers of the Divine care for every human being. From the beginning until the hour of death, human life is surrounded by their constant protection.

It brings many of us such great comfort, knowing that we have so many of God's creatures to reach out to for assistance, guidance, intercession, and companionship as we face the challenges and obstacles our lives can bring.

Over my twenty years as a priest and pastor, I have made many life-giving and long-lasting friendships with many people, including many members of my parish family here at St. Mary's. My previous assignments around the country have also led to many new friends and companions. I am so thankful to God for bringing into my life so many wonderful, loving, caring friends who have impacted my life in so many ways.

I am also grateful for being born into a loving family of two very special parents (Robert and Teresa) and five great siblings (Ginny, Eileen, Bob, Diane, and Joe) who themselves have widened my circle of blessings by bringing into my world several nieces and nephews, some of whom are now married and bringing the next generation of loved ones into our ever-increasing family.

> *Prayer:* "O most faithful companion, whom God has appointed to watch over me, my guide and my protector, ever at my side. What thanks can I offer you for your love, constancy, and protection?
>
> You watch over me in sleep; console me in sorrow; raise me when I fall; ward off

danger; prepare me for the future; withdraw me from sin; urge me to do good, and move me to do penance, and reconcile me with my God.

Thank you for your assistance, and may I never forget your presence. Please, continue to encourage me in adversity, protect me in danger, and assist me in temptations, lest at any time I yield to them. Offer the Divine Majesty all my prayers and sighs and works, and obtain for me the grace to die in the friendship of God, and so to enter into life eternal. Amen." (*The Catholic Prayer Book and Manual of Meditations*)

Scripture for meditation

"Calling the Twelve to him, he began to send them out two by two and gave them authority over impure spirits" (Mark 6:7).

"Faithful friends are a sturdy shelter; whoever finds one finds a treasure" (Sirach 6:14).

"Two are better than one: They get a good wage for their toil. If one falls, the other will help the fallen one. But woe to the solitary person! If that one should fall, there is no other to help" (Eccles. 4:9–10).

Chapter Fifteen

The Final Journey

> For over a thousand years, Roman conquerors returning from the wars enjoyed the honor of triumph, a tumultuous parade. In the procession came trumpeters, musicians, and strange animals from conquered territories, together with carts laden with treasure and captured armaments.

The conquerors rode in a triumphal chariot, the dazed prisoners walking in chains before him. Sometimes his children robed in white stood with him in the chariot or rode the trace horses. A slave stood on the chariot behind the conqueror holding a golden crown and whispering in his ear a warning: "Memento Mori" (remember that you will die!) (General George S. Patton Jr.).

We are all confronted by our mortality at times, particularly as we age. Many of us look back and wonder if we have made the right choices and decisions, taken the right actions, used the right words, and made an effort to become the men and women God created us to be. Over the years, I have visited many people, who were coming to the end of their earthly journey, Some in hospitals, others in hospice care at their homes, and Some in prisons and nursing homes. I have heard confessions in which people have expressed some very sobering profound concerns, such as "Did I live a life pleasing in the eyes of God and my family."

Those who have seen the extraordinary film, *Saving Private Ryan*, may remember the very moving scene, in which Captain John Miller played by Tom Hanks has been mortally wounded after being shot on a bridge during the final battle in Ramelle. Before breathing his last, Captain Miller looks up at the young Private James Ryan played by Matt Damon and whispers these words, " Earn this James! Earn it!"

Captain Miller, along with several of his men, had all given their lives in an attempt to save the life of Private James Ryan and return him home safely to his mother, who has already lost four of her sons in the war.

In the final scene of the film, which takes place in Normandy at the American Cemetery and Memorial, James Ryan is now a much-older man in his seventies, confronted by his own mortality. He is standing alongside his wife and family in front of a marble cross headstone etched with the name of Capt. John Miller. James turns to his wife with tears in his eyes and asks her two important questions: "Am I a good man. Have I led a good life.

Ryans wife reassures him with an emphatic, "Yes!"

The Final Journey

Private Ryan has never forgotten what Captain Miller told him on that fateful day. After that day on the bridge, Ryan tried to live a life that several men lay down their lives to preserve. He truly wanted to "earn it!"

One year while on retreat at the Serra retreat house in Malibu, California, I rented a car and decided to take a drive along the beautiful Pacific Coast Highway. Among the many memorable sites I visited was the "Lone Cypress Tree," a popular place for tourists, photographers, and romantics alike. The Lone Cypress Tree, located near Pebble Beach, sits on a cliff, majestically stretching its gnarled weather-beaten branches out over the blue Pacific Ocean.

The 250-year-old Lone Cypress has been scarred and shaped by fierce Pacific Coast rains and winds. It has taken on a mythical quality. It is among the most photographed trees in North America. At the base of the tree, there was a plaque placed there by an anonymous visitor. The plaque was inscribed with a short verse that reads: "It is not so clear in our living shown which way the winds of change have blown." The poem is a wonderful analogy of our journey. Just as the winds and storms have shaped the lone cypress, giving it character and beauty, our own lives have been shaped by the winds and storms of life.

I remember reading a bumper sticker on the car in front of me while I was stuck in traffic. It read "live yours for your eulogy, not your legacy," *a very sobering message* I thought at the time. I often wonder how many people approach their journey through life in such a way. Several parables come to mind when I reflect on the final leg of ones journey, such as the rich young man who couldn't let go of his earthly possessions in order to follow Jesus or the Parable of the Talents. (XXX 25:14–30), the Parable of the Rich Fool (Luke 12:16–21), the Sower and the Seed (Mark 5:1–20), the Pearl of Great Price (Matt. 13:45–46), and many others. All should remind us to live a life that will make for a eulogy that will be pleasing to the ears of God.

The parable that often gives me pause for some inner reflection is the Parable of Lazarus and the Rich Man.

For those of you who may be unfamiliar with the story:

> *There was a rich man, who was clothed in purple and fine linen and who feasted sumptuously every day. And at his gate lay a poor man named Lazarus, full of sores, who desired to be fed with what fell from the rich*

man's table; moreover, the dogs came and licked his sores. The poor man died and was carried by the angels to Abraham's bosom. The rich man also died and was buried, and in Hades, being in torment, he lifted his eyes and saw Abraham far off and Lazarus in his bosom. And he called out, "Father Abraham, have mercy upon me, and send Lazarus to dip the end of his finger in water and cool my tongue; for I am in anguish in this flame." But Abraham said, "Son, remember that you in your lifetime received your good things, and Lazarus in like manner evil things; but now he is comforted here, and you are in anguish. And besides all this, between you and us, a great chasm has been fixed, in order that those who would pass from here to you may not be able, and none may cross from there to us." "And he said, "Then I beg you, father, to send him to my father's house, for I have five brothers, so that he may warn them, lest they also come into this place of torment." But Abraham said, "They have Moses and the prophets; let them hear them." And he said, "No, father Abraham; but if someone goes to them from the dead, they will repent." He said to him, "If they do not hear Moses and the prophets, neither will they be convinced if someone should rise from the dead." (Luke 16:19–31)

The Life of Our Lord, a book written by Charles Dickens (1846–1849), was not originally intended to be a published work; it was a version of the life of Christ that Dickens wrote so his children could more readily understand and learn to love and enjoy. While studying the Bible for his research, Dickens revisited many of the wonderful parables of the gospels. It has been said that the Parable of Lazarus and the Rich Man was most likely the basis for Dickens masterful work, *A Christmas Carol*. In the classic novel, we find the ghost of Jacob Marley, the infamous symbol of a life wasted on selfish pursuits with little or no thought of his fellow man or his own salvation. He visits Ebeneezer Scrooge and warns him that he is on the same path of a selfish, egocentric path of self-destruction and an afterlife of eternal punishment. Following the visits of the three ghosts, in the novel, Scrooge is given a chance to turn his life around. In the final chapter, Scrooge will give voice to his own repentance and conversion of heart:

> "I will honor Christmas in my heart and try to keep it all the year. I will live in the Past, the Present, and the Future. The Spirits of all Three shall strive within me. I will not shut out the lessons that they teach."

The Final Journey

The promise to change his life for the better has inspired many readers of the classic novel to do the same.

Like Scrooge, there are many who are on the road to perdition! If we find ourselves traveling along such a road, we all have an opportunity while we still have breath in our lungs to change our ways and to conform our hearts and minds to that of Jesus.

Whether it is a showing a preferential option for the poor through works of charity, being a better wife and mother or father and husband, answering the call to follow Jesus as a priest or religious, or praying for the healing of those who are suffering, all these commitments will put us on the path toward salvation!

The Church often reminds us that we are mortal, and our true home is the one that awaits us after we pass from this world. We don't often think of it, but the theme of our final journey is woven throughout our liturgy, our prayers and devotions, our stained-glass windows, statues, and especially in the image of Christ crucified, which is displayed in churches throughout the world. One of our most recited prayers, the Hail Mary, reminds us of our mortality every time we pray it: "Holy Mary, Mother of God, pray for us sinners now and at the hour of our death. Amen." In every Mass, we pray for the deceased, and when we recite the Nicene Creed during mass, we affirm our belief in "...the resurrection of the body and the life of the world to come. The great prayer that Jesus taught us, the "Our Father," which is also prayed at every mass, reminds us that His kingdom will come.

Death can be a scary notion, not knowing exactly what will happen to us. Yet, the saints understood that death was not the end but the beginning of a new life—a belief that we should embrace. Until the time of our departure, we are called to use our gifts and talents to meet the needs and concerns of the poor and the marginalized and for God's greater glory!

Before my beloved father Robert passed away from prostate cancer in January 2006, I would try to drive home from Lowell, Massachusetts, where I was assigned at the time, to be with him and my family on Long Island. As my father declined in his health, I was very blessed to be able to celebrate the mass at the home I grew up in. My mother would repurpose a table in our living room into an altar, and I would use the chalice and patten that my parents gave me at my ordination for the celebration of the Mass. During Thanksgiving and Christmas of that year, my parents, my siblings, and my nieces and nephews would gather in the living room, with my dad sitting in his armchair right next to our makeshift altar. It was so special in so many ways! Having the real presence of Jesus right in the family home where we were raised was such a gift. During the sign of peace, the whole family would warmly hug and kiss each other as we circled the room. We would each lean into Dad as he sat and give him a loving hug and kiss, letting him know how blessed we were to have him as a husband, father, and grandfather.

Eventually, my dad would be placed on hospice care and would spend more time in bed. During one Mass, I consecrated one extra host, which I placed in a pix. When my dad would sleep, I would rest the pix containing the real presence of Jesus on my dad's chest. I felt so comforted as I watched the pix rise and fall with his breathing. We also placed a CD player at his bedside and played Gregorian chants and other music to help create an environment of peace as my dad rested. When Robert finally passed on a chilly January afternoon, one day after we ushered in the new year of 2006, he was surrounded by love, and he indeed did receive the grace of a happy death. At the Mass of Christian burial for my father, the first reading I chose with my mother was the following:

> *Then I saw "new heaven and a new earth," [a] for the first heaven and the first earth had passed away, and there was no longer any sea. I saw the Holy City, the new Jerusalem, coming down out of heaven from God, prepared as a bride beautifully dressed for her husband. And I heard a loud voice from the throne saying, "Look! God's dwelling place is now among the people, and he will dwell with them. They will be his people, and God himself will be with them and be their God. He will wipe every tear*

*from their eyes. There will be no more death'[b]
or mourning or crying or pain, for the old order
of things has passed away."* (Rev. 21:1–4)

It was a reminder that my father was now home after his long journey.

A few years ago, I saw an extraordinary movie titled, *Master and Commander: The Far Side of the World*. The film is set during the naval campaign of the Napoleanic war. The *H.M.S. Surprise*, a British Man of War ship commanded by the brash Captain Jack Aubrey, played by Russell Crowe, is ordered to hunt down and capture a powerful, far-superior French vessel, *The Acheron*, off the South American coast. Though Napoleon is winning the war and the crew members of the "Surprise" face an onslaught of obstacles, including their own internal conflicts, Captain Aubrey is determined that nothing will stop the *Surprise* from completing its mission of defeating the *Acheron* in battle. Before the final battle with the *Acheron*, Aubrey gathers his men on deck and tells them the following: "England is under threat of invasion, and though we be on the far side of the world, this ship is our home. This ship, is England." I found these lines to be very moving. I found that line to be very moving. It is a line that I believe can be adapted to our own journey of faith.

No matter where we may find ourselves in this world we only need invoke Jesus in prayer, and He will come to our assistance and will once again find rest in our true home!

Prayer: "Eternal rest, grant unto him (her) O Lord and let perpetual light shine upon him (her). May he (she) rest in peace (Amen) May their souls and the souls of all the faithful departed, through the mercy of God, rest in peace. Amen."

Scripture for meditation

"Jesus said to her, 'I am the resurrection and the life. The one who believes in me will live, even though they die.'" (John 11:25)

*"Then he said, 'Jesus, remember me when you come into your kingdom.' **43** Jesus answered him, 'Truly I tell you, today you will be with me in paradise.'"(Luke 23:42–43)*

"Do not let your hearts be troubled. You believe in God; believe also in me. My Father's house has many rooms; if that were not so, would I have told you that I am going there to prepare a place for you? And if I go and prepare a place for you, I will come back and take you to be with me that you also may be where I am." (John 14:1–3)

CPSIA information can be obtained
at www.ICGtesting.com
Printed in the USA
JSHW030910310822
29981JS00003B/13

9 781662 851919